Deep Peac  n chambers of a peace-
saturated l   :hallenging social issues
of justice f   ' recommend this book.
Celebration of Discipline

This book is as vital as it is timely, offering a practical and spiritual
guide to recenter believers in the peace of Christ—a peace that loves
kindness, seeks justice, and renounces all fear.

Dr. Kristin Kobes Du Mez, professor, Calvin
University, and author of *Jesus and John Wayne*

Todd Hunter takes aim at our psyches and our consciences with a
biblical word that goes far beyond a calmed nervous system or a Zen-
like tranquility. This book will help us find peace in these tumultuous
times, even with our frenetic schedules.

Russell Moore, *Christianity Today*

Peace is not about withdrawal from the world; it is not sanctified inac-
tion. It is the posture from which we engage the world confident in the
goodness of God. For those looking for spiritual resources to lead them
through this fractured moment, I highly recommend this book.

Esau McCaulley, assistant professor of New
Testament, Wheaton College

Far from offering a quietist, self-help approach to curing anxiety, *Deep
Peace* is filled with earthy wisdom that comes from a lifetime of following Christ and pastoring and teaching the church. I recommend it
to all who seek to know the God of peace.

Tish Harrison Warren, Anglican priest and
author of *Liturgy of the Ordinary*

With patient, expansive, and incisive reflections, Bishop Todd Hunter
shows us the possibility of living in the peace we were made for. In an
age of deep anxiety, this book is a true gift.

Rich Villodas, lead pastor, New Life Fellowship,
and author of *The Deeply Formed Life*

Deep Peace invites readers on a journey to discover the ultimate path to the biblical concept of peace—*shalom*. My prayer as you read Todd Hunter's book is that your heart will be comforted by the God of all peace and that the Spirit of God will use you to be a bearer of peace to a troubled world.

Ed Stetzer, Wheaton College

I am so pleased that Todd Hunter has written this book when so many are crying out for peace between nations, between people, and in the human heart.

Nicky Gumbel, vicar, Holy Trinity Brompton, and pioneer of The Alpha Course

I am thrilled with Todd Hunter's new book! It maps out such a clear path to inner and outer peace with "doable, guilt-free spiritual practices" for growing as persons of peace who bring peace to the world we share together.

Ruth Haley Barton, founder, Transforming Center, and author of *Sacred Rhythms*

Deep Peace is broad in its coverage, deep in its insight, and practical in its wisdom. It is calming medicine for the soul, and I highly recommend it.

J. P. Moreland, professor of philosophy, Talbot School of Theology, Biola University, and author of *Finding Quiet*

In a world where social media does all it can to reconfigure our brains into consumers of outrage, Bishop Todd Hunter calls us to peace with God, with self, and with others. Slow down, give peace a chance, and watch this wise leader set a new pace for peace.

Rev. Canon Dr. Scot McKnight, professor of New Testament, Northern Seminary

It's been said in the past 3,400 years, humans have experienced global peace for just 268 of them. Bishop Todd Hunter addresses many of the reasons why peace has been elusive, where it flows from, and how we can move toward it.

AJ Sherrill, lead pastor, Saint Peter's Church, and author of *Being with God*

Peace is a dovetailing dove that connects spares and splits, heals scars and sores, and nests them into constellations of glowing stars and glorious songs of harmonious difference. This book deserves to sunbathe in every bookshop window and occupy pride of place on every theology shelf.

Leonard Sweet, bestselling author, professor, and founder of PreachTheStory.com and The Salish Sea Press

This deep and moving book shows us how to receive and move through the world with transformative peace—a true gift that will speak to and still many anxious hearts.

Jon Tyson, Church of the City, and author of *The Intentional Father*

As I was reading *Deep Peace*, I felt a quiet calmness come over me. This is no self-help book. Page after page points us to the Prince of Peace, to Jesus himself, who alone can give us peace. Todd Hunter has written many wonderful books, but this is his best writing and thinking yet.

James Bryan Smith, author of *The Good and Beautiful God*

Deep Peace draws with wisdom and compassion the ways Jesus can still our individual and collective storms and give us peace for life in the midst of the storms.

Mark Labberton, president, Fuller Theological Seminary

Todd Hunter is at home in the deep end of the pool, and I'm so excited about his latest work. Has there ever been a timelier resource for the times in which we live?

J. D. Walt, president and sower-in-chief, Seedbed

The peace Todd Hunter opens up for us is not merely individual, but corporate; not merely personal, but prophetic; not merely isolation from a culture in conflict, but full engagement in the world. This is a timely and helpful book as we navigate the peculiar challenges of what it means to embody God's peace in this cultural moment.

Timothy C. Tennent, president, Asbury Theological Seminary, and professor of world Christianity

In an anxious and divided world, Bishop Todd Hunter comes alongside us with gentleness and wisdom. Bringing his considerable experience as both a leader and a shepherd who cares for souls, he helps us diagnose the problem and recognize the cure.

Rev. Dr. Glenn Packiam, associate senior pastor, New Life Church, and author of *Blessed Broken Given*

As leaders we can't even begin to manage the anxiety and fear in the people we lead when we don't know how to manage it in ourselves. *Deep Peace* offers a hopeful vision of life that is a breath of fresh air for all of us trying to live with hope in a busy world.

Jay Pathak, national director, Vineyard Churches USA

Where have all the peacemakers gone? Todd Hunter is a voice crying in the wilderness, calling the church to rediscover deep peace for an anxious world.

Dr. Winfield Bevins, director of church planting, Asbury Seminary, and author of *Ever Ancient, Ever New*

At a time of deep conflict between warring ideologies and racial and generational tensions—both inside and outside the church—the time is right for this important book.

Gary W. Moon, founding executive director, Martin Institute and Dallas Willard Center at Westmont College, and author of *Apprenticeship with Jesus*

Todd Hunter shoots down the idea of peace as being dull and numbed out and instead invites us into a courageous, confident peace in ordinary moments. In response to such hearty, tangible peace, I say, "Bring it on!"

Jan Johnson, author of *Living a Purposeful Life* and president of Dallas Willard Ministries

I cannot imagine a timelier book than this one for our anxious and troubled age. This is *the* book for the fearful, the worried, the angry, the lonely, the truculent, egotistical, disconsolate, and disoriented—which all of us are at some point in our lives. It deserves to be read prayerfully.

W. David O. Taylor, associate professor of theology and culture, Fuller Theological Seminary, and the author of *Open and Unafraid*

DEEP PEACE

FINDING CALM IN A WORLD OF
CONFLICT AND ANXIETY

TODD HUNTER

ZONDERVAN REFLECTIVE

Deep Peace
Copyright © 2021 by Todd D. Hunter

Requests for information should be addressed to:
Zondervan, *3900 Sparks Dr. SE, Grand Rapids, Michigan 49546*
Seedbed Publishing, *415 Bridge Street, Franklin, Tennessee 37064*

Zondervan titles may be purchased in bulk for educational, business, fundraising, or sales promotional use. For information, please email SpecialMarkets@Zondervan.com.

ISBN 978-0-310-12045-2 (audio)

Library of Congress Cataloging-in-Publication Data

Names: Hunter, Todd D., 1956- author.
Title: Deep peace : finding calm in a world of conflict and anxiety / Todd Hunter.
Description: Grand Rapids : Zondervan, 2021.
Identifiers: LCCN 2021016951 (print) | LCCN 2021016952 (ebook) | ISBN 9780310120438 (paperback) | ISBN 9780310120445 (ebook)
Subjects: LCSH: Peace of mind—Religious aspects—Christianity. | Anxiety—Religious aspects—Christianity.
Classification: LCC BV4908.5 .H86 2021 (print) | LCC BV4908.5 (ebook) | DDC 248.4--dc23
LC record available at https://lccn.loc.gov/2021016951
LC ebook record available at https://lccn.loc.gov/2021016952

Cover design: Brand Navigation
Cover images: Freepik
Interior design: Sara Colley

Printed in the United States of America

21 22 23 24 25 26 27 28 29 30 31 32 /LSC/ 12 11 10 9 8 7 6 5 4 3 2 1

TO THE NEXT GENERATION

MY CHILDREN
Jonathan and Carol

My Nieces and Nephews

Julie (Jim) Billings   *Katie Hunter*

Denise (Marc) Terrazas   *Alexandra Pompa*

John (Missy) Hunter   *John (Geanette) Trumbull*

Michelle (Mark) Lee   *Stephanie (Bryan,*

Dennis (Kristy) Hunter   *"BC") Chamberlain*

Melinda (Greg) Bryant   *Emily (Eric) Shrum*

Ryan (Alicia) Hunter   *Jessica (Steve) Reigel*

Jared Hunter   *Chas (Allee) Hogg*

Travis Hunter   *Davis (Megan) Hogg*

May you and your children experience life
at peace with God,
at peace within,
and at peace in the world.

CONTENTS

PEACE WITH OTHERS

PRACTICING PEACE

INTRODUCTION

Through the heartfelt mercies of our God,
God's Sunrise will break in upon us . . .
Then showing us the way, one foot at a time,
down the path of peace.

Luke 1:78–79 MSG

University classes were done for the day, and baseball practice was about to start. As I finished putting on my uniform, I noticed my cleats were not in my locker. Hoping I had left them in the car, I slipped on my flip-flops and rushed out to the stadium parking lot. Out of the corner of my eye, I nervously saw my teammates as they stretched and warmed up. There was nothing in the back seat and nothing in the trunk. I desperately retraced my original steps into the locker room, hoping that the cleats had fallen out of my travel bag. Nothing. Now panic was setting in. I was going to be late—and Coach did not tolerate tardiness. The expectation, always, was to be early, just in case.

What to do? Try to borrow cleats? No time—and all of my buddies were already on the field. Go out to practice in street shoes? Mocking trash talk would have followed. A fellow player rushed past me toward the field and teased me about being late.

He taunted me: "Being late in spring practice is a good way to get cut from the team." I fumed inside and said a few unwritable things to him. Then with my heart pounding, my body thrashing away, and my mind whirling . . . I woke up.

I have had that dream many hundreds of times. As I write, I am a full forty years removed from college baseball. But I still have that dream. In the dream, I am intensely fearful of getting cut from the team, because when I was a young man, baseball was my whole identity. My frustration and anger easily boil over into either begging for help or being in conflict with anyone who enters the dream. Anxiety breeds a corresponding agitation. I have to do something to figure out the problem. If paths toward solutions are blocked, I can feel trapped, and the irritation gets worse.

Peace has not come easy to me. I came into this life wired for worry and anxiety. Something deep in my subconscious comes out in those night terrors. My dearly loved mom often teased me, even as a very young boy, about my propensity to worry. I have spent the last forty-five years trying to address it.

In our days, church leaders and their congregations are plagued by anxiety. Most people are consumers of, and thereby victims of, fear-based, anxiety-producing echo chambers on social media, cable television, and talk radio. It is eating us up from the inside out. To live together well, humans have created social contracts—religious, political, economic, health care, and so forth. All of these now seem to be up for grabs. The future looks muddy.

Christians often feel trapped and powerless to model for the world a peaceful, peace-giving life. This book is meant to provide a map to this peace. It moves readers from encountering the Christ of peace to receiving his peace, to experiencing the deep wholeness that comes from the peace of God, to realizing the outcome of such peace—a life of awakened discipleship for the sake of others.

You may have picked up this book because you suffer from anxiety.[1] You may feel mentally trapped or emotionally suffocated. You know the inner pain and relational conflict that are caused by fretfulness. Like me, you probably have a vision of and a desire for moving from the troubled waters of anxiety to the deep wells of peace. I'll bet you also want to work for a more peaceful and just world. My hope is that this book will be a place where your most profound sources of anxiety are nonjudgmentally named and explained—and you are given a pathway to freedom that empowers you to be a peace-giving, peacemaking person.

What Is Peace?

In our work here, we will explore peace through a Christian and biblical point of view. In the lived experience of our ancient forebearers in faith, peace is understood as:

- completeness
- soundness
- wholeness
- contentment and a prevailing sense of welfare
- an interior marked by quiet as opposed to noisy conflict

Peace comes from being in the care of another—as in, "The LORD is my shepherd" (Psalm 23:1).

Completeness is the positive aspect of peace that heals us from always needing to strive after the one magical thing or person that will finally satisfy us. *Soundness* is the feature of peace that yields a sense of strength rather than the feeling that our minds and bodies are cracking up or falling apart. *Wholeness* is felt as a settled ease, harmony, and general well-being. *Contentment* is a wonderful facet of peace that frees us from the tyranny of disordered desires. *Welfare* is the feeling of security and happiness. *Mental and emotional quiet* as opposed to soul noise is the gift of peace.

As a general introduction, peace describes well-being in the widest sense of the word.[2] Peace refers to health, flourishing, and security. It includes freedom from strife.[3] Peace has to do with salvation—especially as rescue and deliverance. Peace assists right relationships and integrity.[4] It comes from trusting that we are cared for. Peace comes from finding fulfillment or completion of our humanity in Christ, our gifts, and our callings.

There are also missional and justice components of peace that express the mission, character, gospel, and purpose of Jesus.[5] The whole Christian mission is a grand peacemaking endeavor![6] Peace can describe "both the content and goal of all Christian preaching, the message itself called 'the gospel of peace' (Eph 6:15; cf. Acts 10:36; Eph 2:17)."[7]

Peace is deeply personal. It facilitates rest, which results in confidence in and abandonment to God wherein we cease striving to control outcomes. We can do this when the core outcome of our lives is already determined in Christ. We then have no need to justify ourselves to God or others. *Even when struggle is real, there need not be unnecessary struggle in me.* With genuine trust in the greatness and goodness of God, we may need to resist others or things, but we don't have to *make*, through anger and hatred, things come out right.

Peace is also relational and communal. The well-being that comes from a right relationship to God creates persons of peace, whose peace then overflows to others. "Peace is neither the Stoic's withdrawal from the world nor a pious flight into spirituality and mystical contemplation. It is the joyful assurance of sharing already the peace of God as one goes through life and looks to eternity."[8]

Peacefulness refers to qualities of being that are not contentious or quarrelsome, but rather inclined or disposed to avoid strife or dissension. Peacefulness describes persons who are not argumentative or hostile; rather, they are positive and calm, serene and undisturbed. Such persons have an inner stillness that is free from impulses to conflict or disorder.

As much as we all would like to live with and in these qualities of peace every day, smack in our faces are many reasons to *worry*. Worry enough, and *anxiety* sets in. In certain cases, *fear* kicks in. If the presenting concern is strong enough, it becomes a rationale for all manner of soul- and society-destroying attitudes, words, and actions.

My Passion for *Peace*

Because of the daily barrage of negative, overwhelming, and anxiety-inducing news and social media at this turbulent time, people are desperate for peace and goodwill. The problems and challenges of the world (race, politics, economics) far outstrip our moral, ethical, and relational capabilities to respond. This sense of desperation is at the root of all forms of violence, from war to everyday cutting remarks. Emotional cruelty is readily seen on social media and in the "comments" sections of news articles. In the hostile days in which we live, it is not uncommon to feel like the psalmist:

> Too long have I lived
> > among those who hate peace.
> I am for peace;
> > but when I speak, they are for war.
> > > PSALM 120:6–7

Several factors underlie and animate this heartbreaking reality. Some people feel the need to win at all costs; others feel the need to posture their self in a certain way. Un-peace can come from the urge to strongly express one's political or theological views. This is especially true when we do so without the sincere heart desire to listen to or consider the perspective of another. Some of us lash out in conflict because of the need to express relational hurts or rehearse moments of being slighted or trapped by social or economic realities or by workplace or family tensions.

These things are all real. And the associated injustices should be called out.[9] However, these behaviors are also the bedrock justification for our current peace-bankrupt social discourse. The thinking often goes like this: *Something in the world, in my world, is horribly wrong. This wrongness means something should be done. This "something" can include all manner of violence, because, consciously or not, the end justifies the means.*

Such justifications mean that human interaction is far too often marked by anger, meanness, and disrespect. Gone are conversation partners from whom we can learn, grow, and find new perspective. In place of such discourse, I observe an alarming pattern of dismissing, dividing from, condemning, or hating people. Conversation partners are no longer wrong or misinformed; they are evil and dehumanized and made objects of ridicule.

This harmful social discourse does not arise out of the blue. It comes mostly from fear or disordered desires and is found in every place of human endeavor. Most people rationalize toxic discourse by harshly blaming and severely denigrating the person or group they disagree with. It would be good for us all to learn something: such ruthlessness does not find its rationale *out there* in my dumb, evil friend or family member, but *in here*—in my mind, heart, thought life, and emotions; in the current structure of my desires; and in my fear-based, anxious need to control outcomes, to win at all costs.

Given all this, peace appears to be impossible, to be just the wish dream of activists, pacifists, artists, and mystics. Peace seems weak. Contentious resentment, anger, and rage seem strong—the way to really get things done, to get one's way, to make one's point. But as humanity gives itself increasingly to combative forms of discourse, I observe people wondering, *Is this all going too far?* People who spend time on Twitter and Facebook or who tremble at the thought of conflict at family gatherings are now beginning to consider the virtue of peace and to seek it. This book aims to blow fresh air on the embers of peace seeking.

Next Steps

As we move along together in this book, you will find grounding concepts and peace-producing practices for putting anxiety and conflict in their place. I'm confident that as you stay with me, you will find freedom from the grip of worry, fear, and interpersonal battles. I hope to help you see your most profound sources of anxiety and to name them and find explanation for them. I aim to give you a pathway to freedom that facilitates gaining the habits of a peace-giving person. In these pages, we will work together to discover a path away from anxiety toward a life of peace. We will seek to find a spacious, generous, generative life. We will learn practices that alleviate anxiety and promote peace, with the goal of becoming peaceful, just persons in families, churches, neighborhoods, schools, and workplaces.

When all is said and done and this world finally finds its true expression in God, peace will win. Anxiety and conflict will be defeated. Peace from the heart for the sake of others is the destiny of humanity. Heartened by that vision, we simply want to get in alignment *now* with what will be true *then*. We want to sow for a great awakening of peace.

This book does not explore the issues of peace and war or peace and conflict resolution. But our work together will not be complete if we don't spend a bit of time thinking about the social dimension of peace. The God of peace is alive and working in the world too. Noticing and cooperating with his presence and peace-producing activity in ordinary life are the keys to being at peace for the sake of the world. We'll explore this later in the book.

Each chapter concludes with doable, guilt-free spiritual practices for growing as a person of peace. I invite you to get started with the introductory questions below.

As we move into the first section of the book, we will examine ten common peace killers. My goal is to help you recognize, name, and respond to common human issues that push peace away. Chapter 1 focuses on everyday feelings and temptations. Chapter 2 highlights points of personal discomfort. Chapter 3 focuses on external peace robbers.

For now, let's use these questions to get ourselves in tune with our work together.

Peace with God: Does God seem displeased or distant? If so, how might you adjust your relationship to him? Would it involve shifting your attitude? Seeking forgiveness? Picking up a particularly edifying spiritual practice?

Peace Within: What are your challenges with regard to peace within? What do you hope will happen within you as you read this book? See if you can name some goals.

Peace for the Sake of the World: Imagine yourself at peace with God and at peace within. How could such peace facilitate the good you wish to do in the world?

TEN PEACE KILLERS

CHAPTER 1

PEACE KILLERS: FEAR, ANGER, AGGRESSION, ATTACHMENTS

Calm me, O Lord, as You stilled the storm.
Still me, O Lord, keep me from harm.
Let all the tumult within me cease.
Enfold me, Lord, in Your peace.

NORTHUMBRIA COMMUNITY,
"THE FELGILD COMPLINE"

My flower beds are a source of mystery. Why are beautiful flowers harder to grow than weeds? Weeds, like anxiety and conflict, seem to have a robust life of their own. Peace, like flowers, needs tender care. When I've had enough of the frustration, I can always dig up the bed or just let the weeds take over. We may try to carefully cultivate peace, but life has a way of growing weeds that kill our peace.

Unless we're riding a roller coaster or viewing a high-action movie, feeling out of control is no fun. It reminds me of times when I had to travel frequently. I felt like a hamster confined to plastic tubes and a rotating wheel. The relentless "car/shuttle/security/plane/shuttle/rental car line/long meeting" grind—only to do it all again on the way home!—would lead to moments when *fear* would sneak up on me: "Will life ever feel peaceful again?" Or *anger*: "Why is this traffic so bad? Why is this line so long?" *Aggression* would well up as people took too long to get out of the way at the baggage carousel. My strong *attachments* to home and its accompanying routines would leave me frustrated.

Fear, anger, aggression, and attachments—let's take a moment to look more deeply at these persistent peace killers.

Fear

Fear is not a bad thing. Humanity needs fear and its associated feelings of "gut-level apprehension" in order to navigate and survive in a world we're constantly trying to come to terms with. Genuine unease can be felt, whether the perceived threat is real or imagined. But fear also has a psychological effect. It is unsettling and distressing. The feeling of being unsafe, of being threatened by or in danger from a person, setting, or institution, is a common motivator of anti-peace, of lashing out at others.

Sometimes we freeze in the face of fear, while other times we flee the context that could cause us harm. In cases of daily fear, the three most common reactions—fight, flight, or freeze—are not ideal. The goal is to maintain a peacefully responsive rather than a harshly reactive presence.

Insecurity is a form of fear. It is poised to attack most of us every day. Steady, humble confidence is difficult to attain. Worry about what others think of us appears to be universal. Self-doubt is always close by. Past trauma creates insecurity. Trauma exists on a very wide spectrum, but most of us have had plenty of low-grade trauma—at least enough to produce low-grade insecurity. Common sources of insecurity are failure and rejection, scary social situations, and an inner critic that accuses us of being less than perfect.

The un-peace of fear is an appropriate reaction to certain situations. But fear can be indulged so often that it becomes *who we are*. Fear is unhealthy when it becomes a dangerous bit of software or an operating system running in the recesses of our soul. This type of generalized fear, when it programs the GPS directions of our lives, produces all manner of acting out. Cussing people out, flipping them the bird, making cruel judgments, and dismissing people out of hand are just a few common examples.

Yet there is a healthy way to deal with fear so that, ironically, the fear becomes the basis for a deeper peace. First, *name the fear*. Naming it defangs it. Bringing fear out of the dark is a necessary reality check. We cannot deal with shadows; we can only deal with reality. Naming our fear gives us power and authority over it. In naming fear, we can also talk to others about it and receive prayer for it. We see it for what it is—real, but not ultimate or determinative. God's peace is foundational and decisive.

A second way to combat peace-defeating fear is to *take hold of the promises of God*. Meditate on them in such a way that they become a part of you. Picture over and over again the truth that even if you pass through the valley of death, God is with you (Psalm 23:4–5). Use your imagination to firmly grasp the certainty that Jesus is with you through the fiercest storm (Matthew 8:23–27). Similar to the unconscious trust you have in your brake or gas pedal, have confidence that "the LORD gives perfect peace to those whose faith is firm" (Isaiah 26:3 CEV). Welcome the person and work of the Holy Spirit, knowing that "the mind governed by the Spirit is life and peace" (Romans 8:6).

Anger

Anger within drives peace out. Sadly, anger is a friend and an ally to many peace-challenged people. Some people cannot imagine doing life without anger as the chief weapon to get their way. Few things kill peace better than habituated anger. What can we do if we are caught in that trap?

Learn to catch yourself—with neutral emotion and genuine spiritual curiosity—in the moment of anger or aggression. Notice what is happening around you. Can you pick up clues to what triggers you? Look inward: Where is the motivation coming from? To whom is your anger directed? Why? What can you learn about yourself, God, and others in this moment?

Learning the ways of Jesus comes through a process similar to any type of learning and personal growth. But it has one significant difference: the presence of God in the person and work of the Holy Spirit. For instance, as a boy trying to learn to shoot free throws in my driveway, I would not quit until I made ten out of ten shots. In all of this practice, I was trying to determine things like the angle of my elbow, the consistent use of my legs, and my posture. Similarly, we pursue peace through spiritual practices, but with awesome power attending us—namely, the person and work of the Spirit (Galatians 5:22–23) actively kneading the fruit of the Spirit (such as peace) into us.

With childlike determination and joy we must engage the process of seeking peace through the process of spiritual transformation. If we don't, defensiveness, posturing, or pretending soon follow. Or debilitating self-talk. Or quitting. That's what I did as a youth when it came to dancing. I judged myself to be so poor at it and so hopeless to get better that I simply refused to dance. That choice had relatively minor consequences. But making such a choice with regard to habitual anger is soul-destroying. It destroys marriages, friendships, and work relationships.

Aggression

Being aggressive sounds like the right posture and practice in the rough-and-tumble of the business world, in a tough athletic contest, and certainly in the arena of a military battle. Fair enough. I recognize that in some settings, being forceful or insistent has its place. But as we pursue peace in the spiritual life, we must cultivate the opposite of aggression—namely, *gentleness*. As Adrian van Kaam writes, "Gentleness is the readiness to quiet down the noise that threatens to cut us off from the voice of the Spirit . . . Gentleness is a preparation for and fruit of [peace]."[1]

When aggressiveness is a person's underlying attitude, what generally follows is strife with others, failure to love others, and a predisposition to fight. Discussions become the context for hostility. Differences with others bring forth a readiness to be argumentative and dismissive.

Sometimes people confuse aggressiveness with *boldness* and *assertiveness*. Though both can be overplayed, they have a more natural place in the spiritual life. Following God often calls for bold moves. The apostles prayed for the ability to teach about Jesus with boldness (Acts 4:29). Paul taught about the kingdom of God—which made the political and religious powers nervous—with boldness (Acts 28:31).

Bringing justice to systems and situations of injustice calls for assertiveness that defeats the status quo. Noah, Abraham, Moses, David, and the prophets; Deborah, Miriam, and Esther; Lydia and Priscilla—all of these modeled assertiveness in an effort to obey God in the face of dual antagonists: their internal misgivings and the social, relational, and political pushback from their contemporaries. Boldness facilitates obedience. Assertiveness can empower forward movement when everything is arrayed against that which is right. We can thank God for both.

But there is a difference between appreciating the usefulness of being bold or assertive and making the leap to embrace aggression as a lifestyle. That is an anti-peace move. We will not have peace within or peace between when every conversation, every board meeting, every talk with a child or spouse, or every simple conflict with a neighbor becomes a setting for rationalized aggression, for getting our way—no matter what it takes.

That attitude is actually a loser in the long term. As soon as people identify others as aggressive, they want nothing to do with them. Kids leave home as fast as they can. Spouses file for divorce. Promotions go to others who don't destroy teamwork.

Think of aggression as a huge, ornery bull that is unrestrained. It may prove useful in the future, but it is much more likely to lead to an accident that harms a loved one. For those who seek peace within and peace between parties, cultivating gentleness is a far more useful and powerful way to go. A godly, gentle person can always grab some assertiveness when they need it—like a chef grabbing a bit of spice off the rack. But a person who is by nature aggressive can rarely pivot to peace.

To those committed to aggressive living, peace is considered weak. And weak means I am not in control, which may mean I don't get what I want. This line of thinking breeds fear, which in turn becomes the deep rationale for aggressive attitudes, words, and behaviors.

In the realm of peace, things work very differently. Veterans of a peaceful interior know that peace, being an attribute of God, is strong. As people not given over to fear, they know their deep internal peace means they don't always have to be in control. Peace-filled persons are not fixated on getting want they want. They are free. Such freedom is the grounds for loving others, not bludgeoning them to get what they want—like an angry person beating and shaking a vending machine in which their coin has just gotten stuck. Humans don't take well to being beaten and shaken, but they thrive in the context of the freedom fueled by gentle peace expressed in love.

Attachments

When possessions become an extension of our self, we have a problem. The anxiety linked to the process of getting and protecting that to which we are attached leads to disordered attitudes that rob our peace.

I had to detach from certain things to find peace. For instance, when I used to play golf, I loved searching for just the right golf club on eBay. I felt butterflies as the seconds wound down on an auction for a shiny new club. Looking back, I also now realize my 1969 Camaro was never going to make me a tough guy. Sitting in it did not change my essential wiring. The Porsche 911 I bought at twenty years old with my own hard-earned money never made me sexy like the stereotypical European male. In junior high school, a Members Only jacket, could my family have afforded one, would not have yielded a true sense of belonging. But attachments to those things did create a stain on my soul. To be rid of that stain has taken years of patient attention.

How then do we find true fulfillment in life? How do followers of Jesus rightly seek satisfaction? How do we detach ourselves from the deeply embedded notion that fulfillment comes from cruises, luxury cars, fine dining, and exotic vacations? What are we to think of the words of Jesus: "Seek first his kingdom and his righteousness, and all these things will be given to you as well" (Matthew 6:33)?

I find valuable the way *The Message* captures the spirit and intent of Jesus' invitation to make the kingdom primary in our lives. It banishes the consumerism that facilitates disordered attachments: "Steep your life in God-reality, God-initiative,

God-provisions. Don't worry about missing out. You'll find all your everyday human concerns will be met" (Matthew 6:33 MSG).

Is there a way to interact with possessions and experiences such that they bring peace, not constant addiction to consumption? I think so. But to get there, we need to ask a couple of questions. *Have we been told the wrong story about the meaning of life? Where is the one place in the Bible or the history of religion where the pursuit of things is the goal of human life?* If we're not living in alignment with God's purpose for humanity, no wonder we are not at peace with him or within ourselves, and thus we are unable to be peacemakers for the world.

Attachments order our lives. Desires organized by God's purposes for humanity will, in general, bring peace. Disordered desires cause all manner of conflict and anxiety. When I feel those things, I have turned for decades to Thomas à Kempis:

> Choose always to have less rather than more. Seek always after the lowest place, and to be subject to all. Wish always and pray that the will of God be fulfilled in thee. Behold, such a man as this entereth into the inheritance of peace and quietness.[2]

In the next chapter, we will expand our knowledge of peace killers. Knowledge is a first step in seeking transformation toward peace.

Peace with God: What practices might you need to employ to "steep your life in God-reality, God-initiative, God-provisions"?

Peace Within: Which peace killer troubles you most—fear, anger, aggression, or attachments? Take a moment to wonder why. Ask God, and if possible a spiritual friend, for some practices for pruning this peace killer to make room for new growth—for peace.

Peace for the Sake of the World: In what ways does the peace killer you named above produce conflict with others? Describe that process and imagine different outcomes. How can you move forward toward those different outcomes?

CHAPTER 2

PEACE KILLERS: PAIN, UNANSWERED PRAYER, SELF-CENTEREDNESS

*Now may the Lord of peace himself give you
peace at all times and in every way.*
2 Thessalonians 3:16

I try exceedingly hard to think right. It is important to me that my beliefs correspond to reality. It feels to me, as a pastor and teacher, that being right is job number one. I don't think of this in an arrogant or self-righteous way. Rather, a correct orientation to reality simply seems fundamental to the good life. When I struggle, groping to find the truth or the right way, I feel a lot of peace-killing discomfort. Let's take some time to think about how elements of discomfort—such as pain, unanswered prayer, and the insecurity that triggers self-centeredness—work against peace.

Pain

Chronic pain is one the most harrowing of all human conditions. I get queasy when I hear about someone going through it. It triggers dread in me, and it shakes me.

God is not mad at you if you have chronic physical pain. Pain simply records in our bodies that we fell off a ladder, got in a car crash, have osteoarthritis, or had something go wrong in a surgery. God is not punishing you; he is with you. God specializes in dealing with deep, persistent pain. He has watched his creation in pain for millennia. He has "tried everything," as we say when dealing with pain. But "in these last days he has spoken to us by his Son" (Hebrews 1:2). This Son, this Word of God, is the final answer to our pain. He is our companion in it, and at the consummation of all things, he will be our final, full healer. But for now, some fifty million Americans deal daily with chronic pain.[1]

As an athlete I was encouraged to deny pain. "Walk it off!" I was told. Many of us heard this from parents or older siblings: "Stop crying right now or I'll give you something to cry about!" Pain then gets attached to shame, to the fear of looking weak to others. Pain is nothing to be ashamed of. Pain does not make you less of a person.

Unrelenting pain is a heavy load to carry. It hinders the ability to focus. We fear it will never go away. We wonder, *Who will I be then? How will I be then? What will life be like? How diminished will my life be?* Projecting into the future, we grieve losses that haven't yet happened. If you have chronic pain, you've likely had people say, "Have you tried . . .?" These well-meaning comments are frustrating. In unrelenting pain, we are simply trying to survive the hour and then the afternoon, with the hope that sleep will come in the evening.

The stress associated with chronic physical pain takes an emotional toll. Hopelessness comes knocking. We feel helpless in the face of an unseen power. Mood and personality changes occur. Our social life all but disappears. We fear that friends and family will get turned off by our "neediness." Depression and suicidal thoughts can follow. We cry foul. *Why me? It's not fair! No one understands what I am going through!* Pain becomes an enemy to fight. Which means that *a fighting spirit* can begin to control us, consuming every thought, feeling, and interaction. Trembling at the thought of having to deal with it myself, I respect everyone who battles chronic physical pain.

Merciless pain creates cruel loneliness and a loss of hope. Pain sufferers long for honest, empathetic support. The companionship of Jesus, of the Spirit, is the source of peace within pain. Jesus endured agony in Gethsemane because of his Father's close presence. Divine presence, Jesus' home in the Trinity, gave him the peace and confidence to move forward into the reality of the indescribable brutality that ensued.

The psalmist assures our quaking hearts that "the LORD is close to the brokenhearted and saves those who are crushed in spirit" (Psalm 34:18). In the words of Jesus, nearness turns to union: a branch in a vine, the life of the vine flowing to the branch—even in storms with whipping winds and bruising hail (John 15:1–17). Companionship and union should not be dismissed as cliché. They produce peace in our hearts, which is then leveraged against the pain in our bodies.

Unanswered Prayer

The virtues of peacefulness and peaceableness are dug from heartache and struggle. And for people learning to follow Jesus, the fear and confusion surrounding unanswered prayer are big challenges to our spiritual peace—fear because we wonder if something is wrong with our prayers, and confusion because we've all been taught that God does indeed answer prayer; otherwise, what's the point of praying?

Jesus, while not turning prayer into magic, put a fine point on the matter: "Whatever you ask for in prayer, believe that you have received it, and it will be yours" (Mark 11:24). The apostle John taught, "This is the confidence we have in approaching God: that if we ask anything according to his will, he hears us. And if we know that he hears us—whatever we ask—we know that we have what we asked of him" (1 John 5:14–15).

But not every prayer is clearly answered. How do we live in peace when our prayers are delayed or unanswered? Paul knew a great deal about asking for relief and not getting it:

> Three times I pleaded with the Lord to take it away from me. But he said to me, "My grace is sufficient for you, for my power is made perfect in weakness." Therefore I will boast all the more gladly about my weaknesses, so that Christ's power may rest on me. That is why, for Christ's sake, I delight in weaknesses, in insults, in hardships, in persecutions, in difficulties. For when I am weak, then I am strong.
>
> 2 CORINTHIANS 12:8–10

Let's dig out some peace from Paul's prayer life.

Biblical scholars disagree about the "it" Paul was asking the Lord to take away. It could have been a physical ailment, a besetting sin, or a habitual reaction to people like the Judaizers, who constantly contradicted Paul's teaching about grace and freedom in Christ. Whatever "it" was, it was painful, and Paul wanted it gone. His prayers went unanswered. But his relationship with God remained. *In* Christ was the place of Paul's peace. Thus, the question shifts from "How can I get what I want in prayer?" to "How can I be in a meaning-making relationship with Christ despite the unfulfilled desire of unanswered prayer?"

When Paul says he "pleaded with the Lord," we get the feeling they sat down and discussed it during a few meetings. Paul, in making his best case, implored his master to take it away. God denied his petition.

Then Jesus says something that could be interpreted as uncaring: "My grace is sufficient for you, for my power is made perfect in weakness." "Uh, Lord," we may be tempted to say back, "I asked for relief, not grace and power to make it through. That's kind of you and all, but I want it gone!" In the end, Paul embraced the Lord's answer as the path to strength, and strength is a close sibling of peace.

In another passage, we see clearly that in spite of Paul's prayer life, hardship was more the rule than the exception:

> We are hard pressed on every side, but not crushed; per-
> plexed, but not in despair; persecuted, but not abandoned;
> struck down, but not destroyed. We always carry around in
> our body the death of Jesus, so that the life of Jesus may also
> be revealed in our body . . . Though outwardly we are wasting
> away, yet inwardly we are being renewed day by day. For our
> light and momentary troubles are achieving for us an eternal
> glory that far outweighs them all. So we fix our eyes not on
> what is seen, but on what is unseen, since what is seen is tem-
> porary, but what is unseen is eternal.
>
> 2 CORINTHIANS 4:8–10, 16–18

The life of Paul conveys several truths. Peace in the midst of unanswered prayer comes to those who look in the right place—to that which is eternal, not momentary. Peace comes to those who learn to see the goodness of God within various kinds of suffering. This truth isn't meant to dismiss or minimize pain or to overspiritualize it. It just means we can only find God in the life we are now living. For many of us, this means finding the goodness of God in regular bouts of pain.

In following the model of Paul, we are delivered from self-accusing feelings of victimization. Along the Pauline path we learn to discern God in our real lives—even as we peacefully pray for the painful parts of our lives to be altered. Prayers, answered or unanswered, should come within an overall conversational relationship with Jesus, such as what you'd imagine between a master teacher and an apprentice. As we wait for an explanation for unanswered prayer, this relational context, with its ongoing conversation, is the context in which peace occurs.

Self-Centeredness

I saw an article recently with the provocative title "Self-Absorption: The Root of All (Psychological) Evil?"[2] The author makes this claim:

> Self-absorbed individuals typically don't show much concern about anyone or anything outside their (narrow) self-interest . . . Obviously, paying attention to our wants and needs is appropriate, even necessary. But whether we're feeling extremely bad or nervous about ourselves, worriedly ruminating about how others perceive us, or indulging in grandiose thoughts about our "specialness," we're descending into a state of toxic self-absorption.[3]

Anxiousness routinely, though not always, comes from self-centeredness. It springs from the thoughts and feelings that what

I need and want in a given situation is what is most important and must be pursued with every means necessary to secure my preferable outcome.

Life bent in that manner twists us away from peace with God and peace within. Peace with others also becomes impossible, since such a life has a toxic spillover into social relationships. The article on self-absorption explains: "From a variety of phobic, anxiety, and obsessive-compulsive impairments to many depressive disturbances, to various addictions, to post-traumatic stress disorder, and to most of the personality disorders, *self-absorption can be seen as playing a major role.*"[4]

Here is the freeing idea that kills self-absorption and fosters peace: "I am not the sum total of my goods or experiences. To be *me* I don't need to taste everything, see everything, or go everywhere. I don't have to look perfect. I find myself in Christ, not in consuming various products, services, entertainments, or experiences." The person at peace knows by experience that Jesus was right—that everyone who drinks from the things of earth (he was talking about water from a well) will predictably thirst again. But as Jesus told the woman with whom he was conversing, "Whoever drinks the water I give them will never thirst." And then he sweetened the deal, saying, "Indeed, the water I give them will become in them a spring of water welling up to eternal life" (John 4:13–14).

Peace comes as the satisfying overflow from having our thirst quenched in Jesus. Using Jesus' analogy, lowering the bucket into the wells of the world over and over to find satisfaction and peace merely creates more anxiety: Will *this* finally be the time my effort pays off? Life begins to seem like the carnival crane game that swings and lowers with a claw to pluck a prize. It almost never works. This sort of life leads to a habitual longing, which in turn generates serious forms of anxiety.

But there is hope. When we are transformed from the

self-centered thinking that life is comprised of getting what we want, we are set free to cultivate simplicity. Uncomplicated living yields peace—the peace that comes from an inward reality of single-hearted focus on God and his kingdom. From this simple, peaceful focus proceeds an outward lifestyle of modesty, openness, and unpretentiousness. In this way we gently discipline our hunger for status, glamour, and luxury.

Jesus is not being religiously narrow-minded when he says, "Seek first his [God's] kingdom" (Matthew 6:33). Jesus is a wise teacher. He is revealing a simple but profound spiritual truth—a truth especially poignant for peace seekers: "No one can serve two masters. Either you will hate the one and love the other, or you will be devoted to the one and despise the other. You cannot serve both God and money" (Matthew 6:24).

If you find yourself in the grip of self-centeredness, you have probably rationalized it in some way: "I deserve this car," or "I need that certain experience." But there is a way to escape this prison—by cultivating thankfulness. Become aware of spaces and places in which you recognize the goodness of God in your day-to-day life.

Paul excelled at this spiritual practice. It facilitated his ministry in the midst of the hardships described above: "I have learned to be content whatever the circumstances. I know what it is to be in need, and I know what it is to have plenty. I have learned the secret of being content in any and every situation, whether well fed or hungry, whether living in plenty or in want" (Philippians 4:11–12).

The secret to slaying self-preoccupation is this: to live in the kingdom of God as an apprentice to Jesus. Following Jesus, trusting his worldview, striving to keep his teaching, desiring to mimic the way he carried himself in the world, will automatically lead us to a healthy focus on the other—family, friends, coworkers, schoolmates, and neighbors. When *the other* is the focus, the anxiety rooted in selfishness diminishes and sometimes even vanishes. We then have a peaceful bearing. People trust us more. Life and ministry become much freer, calmer, and more joyful. As the lovely Taizé chorus proclaims, "The kingdom of God is justice and peace and joy in the Holy Spirit. Come, Lord, and open in us the gates of your kingdom."[5]

As we move in the direction of selflessness, little by little we become consumed with showing our love for God, with serving our neighbors, and with blessing our enemies. The move to God and others is not mostly psychological. It is not an inner temper- ament or skill. It is rooted in confidence in God—that he is, and he has, all we need. If we need Jesus and _____ (fill in the blank), we are constantly vulnerable. "Just needing Jesus" bestows the great gift of a quiet mind not given over to anxiously worrying about ourselves. A peaceful heart comes from resting in the pro- vision of God. Moreover, the one with a settled soul has the best potential to become the person God intended—his cooperative friend for the sake of others.

As we move along together, we will have much more to say about the way that peace overflows to pursue the good of others. In the next chapter, though, we have a few more peace killers to explore.

Peace with God: Does God feel distant from your experience of pain? Have you accused him of neglect? Do you need to let God off the hook? What do you need to do to make a fresh start with God?

Peace Within: What are the sources of your discontent? Does your dissatisfaction spring come from well-ordered or disordered desires? What path can you take to learn "the secret of being content in any and every situation"?

Peace for the Sake of the World: Do you sometimes use others to get what you want—to medicate discomfort? Imagine the people in your life not as sources, vendors, or producers but as objects of your love and service. What kind of change takes place in your heart when you make that adjustment?

CHAPTER 3

PEACE KILLERS: LIFE ONLINE, OBSESSION WITH FAILURE, FEAR OF MISSING OUT

What we decide to seek in life is the key to our character, and further determines what our character will be.

DALLAS WILLARD, "THE
CRAFTINESS OF CHRIST"

We begin to differentiate from our parents at the worst time—middle school and high school. Just when adolescent classmates are becoming particularly mean! The nuclear bombs of this nastiness include being trolled online in a demeaning, hostile, or sexual way; having failures or imperfect body parts pointed out; or developing a deep fear of rejection that stems from not being invited to a party.

Adults experience similar issues. We feel the hatred on Twitter and the rage on Facebook. We fail to achieve promotions or get raises at work. We don't get invited to lunch or to drinks after work. In this chapter, we'll discuss three more peace killers: life online, obsession with failure, and fear of missing out.

Life Online

Partisan politics and the ugly civil discourse that accompanies it are a top peace killer. If someone were to examine the discourse online, on talk radio, and on cable news, they may assume that expressing oneself with rancor, name-calling, and arrogant dismissal of others is the natural and normal mode of human interaction. The issues are important. People on all sides of any debate want and need to be heard. Reasonable people disagree about a wide variety of subjects. Honest conversations about complex issues require subtlety, nuance, and negotiation—not the dropping of verbal bombs or the tweeting of high-powered bullets. Important conversations happen better with calmness, with thinking well about our conversation partners.

In addition to sour discourse, just spending too much time online can poison the soul. Online noise results in a chaotic, swirling mind and screaming emotions. In the early twenty-first century, online racket is a chief cause of anxiety and is a prime peace stealer. But what happens online is not the foundational issue. Twitter does not choose anyone's words. Facebook does not control fingertips as they type. Instagram does not dictate the motives behind posts. Those things come as the overflow of one's interior life—whether it's a calm pool of peace or a cruel pit of hatred.

To be a person of peace online, we must have well-ordered desires that are the fruit of having turned over our entire life to God, abandoning all outcomes to him. We don't have to win every argument. We don't always have to be right. Even when we believe we are right, we can make our case in peace and leave our conversation partner in charge of their own mind. Think about a time when you were wrong about something. Would you have been best moved to rightness by someone trying to control you or by another person making their case and letting you come to your own conclusions?

Well-ordered desires and abandonment are important because harmful civil discourse does not arise in a vacuum. It arises mostly out of fear and disordered desires. These are found in every place of human endeavor. Most people rationalize toxic discourse by blaming and denigrating the person or community they're interacting with. It rarely occurs to us that such ruthlessness does not find its source or rationale *out there*—in my unintelligent, evil friend, family member, or colleague. It finds its source *in here*—in my mind, heart, thought life, and emotions; in the current structure of my desires; and in my fear-based, anxious need to control outcomes, to win at all costs. Our current set of disordered desires is what must change if we are to be consistent agents of peace. Otherwise, people are just objects to *use*, not persons to *love*.

Therefore, the hope for our social discourse is not so much in policy changes enacted by the social media giants as it is in the transformation of our hearts toward gentle peace. Life online will only get better as we trod the pathway to becoming persons immersed in and overflowing with peace. We will find peace in our complex social storms when we no longer let sound bites and tweets frame our view of the world and its problems. As Christ followers, we have our own frame: a personal triune God, his purposes in human history, and the coming fulfillment of that history. Current political persons and ideas are real and are either helpful or harmful. But when they are set against the proper backdrop of the redemption of the whole cosmos and all eternity, they are miniscule, timebound, and temporary. Why then should we let them dictate the rhetoric and imagination of the church and divide us?

To move toward gentle peace, we must recognize that the multifaceted reality of our lives and the cosmic reality of God's purposes for humanity are not contained in most of our explanatory systems: conservative, liberal, fundamentalist, libertarian, Democrat, Republican, or denominational. Yet we all feel the occasional temptation to run back to these familiar categories. We think simple, consistently applied political or religious worldviews will teach us how to live in relation to others. But it is not working. It cannot work. The problem is that explanations of life based on partisan ideology cannot reliably account for current complexities.

Conservatives would never dream it to be the case, but sometimes the left is right—as in *correct*. The reverse is, of course, true as well—which shocks liberals. The big idea here is this: to do well in life online and in various other media, we must always remember that God and *his* redemptive work in humanity cannot be stuffed into a ballot box in the hope that out of the other side will come a public policy that dependably fits God's goals for human life. Our votes sometimes get it right, and for that we should be genuinely thankful. I am not advocating for an overall social cynicism. I'm trying to give you an imagination for being at peace within a setting of angry social discourse—a peace rooted in God's superintending of human history—and thus becoming a person of peace online.

Spiritually healthy approaches to dealing with social media–based conversations come from cultivating *core feelings* such as love, joy, and peace. These are conditions of the soul from which words, decisions, and actions arise. Love, joy, and peace, over the course of time, fostered in fellowship with God, simply crowd out fear, anger, resentment, unsatisfied desire, woundedness, and rejection. Those things lose their power to *trigger* us toward words and actions we regret.

Obsession with Past Failure

I can still remember getting a bad jump on a ball that cost my team a league championship, dropping a pop fly in a key game, and striking out with the game on the line. Even though these memories are almost fifty years old and I know these events don't matter at all in the big picture, I see them and feel them as if they happened last week.

These kinds of events happen in the realm of relationships too. We let someone down. Blow our final chance. Capitulate out of self-preservation. Blurt out something we immediately regret. These failures leave scars in the psyche. Then something happens that scratches those scars, which triggers old thoughts and emotions, which then ruins today and renders tomorrow hopeless. Painful memories grab hold of us as we drive along a quiet road or lie awake in bed at night. Past mistakes or sins emerge as if they are being presented by a prosecuting attorney. We can feel swallowed up by our past or imprisoned by it. The voice of depression can ring out: "I've beaten against the doors. I've cried out for help. But the cinder block and iron bars of my emotional prison don't budge!"

When we don't make peace with the past, it squashes possibilities in the present and stamps out potential in the future. True enough. But can I make peace with my past? In many cases it feels impossible. We wonder, *Will I always be in the grip of painful memories? Do they define my being? Have they embedded themselves in me to the point of ultimate control?*

Having been an athlete and having lived my adult life as a public person, I have a lot of experience with negative self-talk. Rather than telling myself, *I made a poor decision,* I say, *I stink as a leader.* Rather than telling myself, *I said something imprecise in my talk,* I say, *I should never be on a stage again.* Rather than telling myself, *I had an awkward moment in a conversation,* I say, *I'm a horrible person.* Rather than saying, *I made a misjudgment,* I say, *I'm the worst friend ever.*

Maybe your preoccupation with the past comes out something like this:

- *I am stupid*—not, *I made a mistake.*
- *I am a slimy person*—not, *I had a moment of dishonesty.*
- *I am a horrible person*—not, *I'm working to make changes in my life.*
- *I am a deviant*—not, *I gave in to a moment of temptation.*
- *I am destined to* _____ *(fill in the blank)*—not, *I have tendencies to addictive behaviors or pestering sins.*

This merry-go-round of self-accusation takes a long time to slow down. I am working on stopping it. I've learned that our past failures become either learning experiences or debilitating memories. Past experiences either facilitate harmful obsession or become helpful tools for problem solving. Disappointments cannot be undone. But *we* can be transformed by focusing on the present and dreaming of a future that pulls us into others-oriented opportunities to serve.

The shock and grief that occur with trauma—with deeply distressing or disturbing experiences—can have an imprisoning power. Past incidents can lead us to mistrust God. And if we stop to think about it, God may be humanity's biggest disappointment. Everyone has a beef with God. The fall—and the huge tree of evil that has grown from that seed—has consequences for all of us. Death. Robbery. Rape. Racial injustice. Divorce. Injury. Hunger. Sickness. And pain—oh, the pain and disappointment of human life! The repercussions of such events are deeply felt and long-lasting. And so we put God on the witness stand: *Why, God . . . why did you let sin enter the world? Why did you even create us in the first place?*

The Good of Creation Precedes the Evil of the Fall

God's story actually starts before creation, before space and time as we know and experience it. Before creation there was *being*, one being of three persons, our triune God. Within this trinity of Persons are relationship and love. *Relationship* means there was activity before it could be put on a timeline. And along with personhood comes intentionality. God created not haphazardly, not arbitrarily, but with *intention*. We first see his intention for humanity when in the garden narrative he asked the first humans, Adam and Eve, to work with him as his cooperative friends. Then came the fall, with all of its ugly effects throughout human history.

But creation and fall are not all there is to God's story. We must add *telos*. *Telos* is the New Testament word for "completion" or "fulfillment." In the biblical context, this word pointed to the completion of God's intention. *Telos* alerts us to a game-changing, life-altering reality: what God wants done *will* be done. Nothing is going to stop it—not our sins nor our accusations against God's loving goodness and wisdom. In that day, at the completion of all things, at the unveiling of the new heaven and the new earth, God, having made all things right, will be seen for who he is: Intender, Creator, Shaper, Sustainer, Savior, and Completer. In that day, all questions—honest or cynical—cease, and full-sighted, full-hearted, full-throated worship begins.

And we don't have to wait. The healing of *that* day has, in the coming of Jesus and the Holy Spirit, entered *our* day. This means a door lies open before us:

You [must] let the distress bring you to God, not drive you from him. The result [will be] all gain, no loss.

Distress that drives us to God does that. It turns us around. It gets us back in the way of salvation. We never regret that kind of pain. But those who let distress drive them away from God are full of regrets, end up on a death-bed of regrets.

2 CORINTHIANS 7:9–10 MSG

Self-Reflection, Not Obsession

Self-reflection is core to Christian spirituality. Sometimes looking back is painful. But we must be careful not to elevate our transient, self-accusing feelings over the desire of God to express love and forgiveness. Sometimes the effects of sin linger—the DUI results in a lost license, which makes daily life even more challenging; the lie breaks trust, and reestablishing that trust will take time. But these facts are not the same as "God does not forgive me" or "I cannot forgive myself."

Angst over our past is part of the human condition. The unwillingness to forgive ourselves is sometimes a subconscious strategy to enforce our conclusion that we are not a good person or that we deserve pain and shame. But obsession with past failures will kill peace.

The move away from obsession with the past and toward peace is comprised of giving and receiving forgiveness, which brings hope and freedom, which then bring peace. But we may feel stuck in a vicious cycle that spins us around and around: "God has forgiven me, but my thoughts and feelings keep badgering me." We fear that "this thing has become a part of me." Maybe, but if so, it is merely a few bits of electronic data captured in the massive storage of "the cloud." Whatever is torturing you is not the whole you. It is not definitive. Self-incrimination can be swallowed up in the greater reality of God's love, forgiveness, reconciliation, and re-creating power.

> Praise the LORD ... who forgives all your sins and ... who redeems your life from the pit and crowns you with love and compassion, who satisfies your desires with good things ... The LORD is compassionate and gracious, slow to anger, abounding in love ... For as high as the heavens are above the earth, so great is his love for those who fear him; as far as the east is from the west, so far has he removed our transgressions from us.
>
> PSALM 103:2–5, 8, 11–12

> "I will forgive their wickedness and will remember their sins no more."
>
> HEBREWS 8:12

> If we confess our sins, he is faithful and just and will forgive us our sins and purify us from all unrighteousness.
>
> 1 JOHN 1:9

Obsession with past failures is as human as breathing. But we are not limited to that stale, polluted air. The testimony of our ancestors is that the life portrayed by the Scriptures is fresh air available to us, oxygenating our faith and giving hope—from which come peace and the ability to be persons of peace.

Fear of Missing Out

Peace does not flow from fear of any kind, and certainly not from the anxious *fear of missing out*. Peace cannot come from needing to see everything, taste everything, and go everywhere. Craving a certain bit of merchandise or a particular experience produces a restless spirit within us, an agitated mind, and an impatient heart. Susan Muto and Adrian van Kaam write, "The furious pursuit of pleasure steals rest and gentleness; impatient desire prevents abiding peace."[1]

When we impatiently reach for a product-based future, the present moment—the moment in which you, God, and your neighbor reside—is missed. Life can only happen in the present moment. Unbridled seeking of *fulfillment* and uninhibited striving for *satisfaction* are not good guides for life. When they become guides, a few aspects of anti-peace are bound to follow: anxiety, a lack of empathy, a domineering attitude, and various forms of embittered relationships. Just ask the family, friends, and coworkers of people who live this way. They will be able to show you the scars.

In glaring contrast, love for God and for the righteousness, peace, and joy of his kingdom lead to a peace-filled homecoming for the soul. Coming back home to God "is a return to the source, a regaining of the lost core of our lives," writes Ronald Wells.[2] You find deep rest at home. Your own bed, your own pillow, familiar furniture. You are relaxed. You sleep better at home. At home, the food—just the way Mom, Dad, or Grandma made it—tastes better, and its aroma is intoxicating as you sit on a squeaky chair at that old table. The couch feels like a long-lost memory coming back. The family dog jumps in your lap, and childlike joy wells up in you. What home does to your body and its senses is what life in the kingdom of God does for the soul: it puts the soul at rest, so that it both embodies and radiates peace.

This insight sounds completely true: "The kingdom of selfish desires is nothing like the gentle kingdom of God. It is not really a kingdom; it is an anarchy of lust, greed, envy, and anger . . . It is a reign of endless disappointment . . . and lasting dissatisfaction."[3] We have a whole other agenda we are pursuing. We don't live to consume; we merely consume what we need to live. We live out of a different imagination. People at peace are not driven by the fear of missing out, but by what they already have as followers of Jesus—calling, meaning, and purpose for living. Rejecting the fear of missing out, people at peace know this: "Keep it simple—in marriage, grief, joy, whatever. Even in ordinary things—your daily routines of shopping, and so on. Deal as sparingly as possible with the things the world thrusts on you. This world as you see it is fading away" (1 Corinthians 7:30–31 MSG).

You have very likely identified in your own life a few of the peace killers we've discussed. But the news isn't all bad. The things in us that work against peace happen, are carried along, and find their hope in a context—namely, the Trinity of peace. In the next chapter, we begin by paying attention to the God of peace.

Peace with God: Do you spend a lot of time on social media, cable television, or talk radio? After a long session, do you feel closer to God? If not, what can you do to reduce your intake?

Peace Within: Consider the fear of missing out. Does frequent use of social media increase or diminish the anxiety associated with it in you? If social media causes fear of missing out or other forms of anxiety in you, why do you keep at it? What is it you want more than peace within?

Peace for the Sake of the World: Sometimes we feel owned or controlled by the world. See if you can name how that is true for you. What steps can you take to free yourself so you can become an agent of love, peace, and justice in the world?

A TRINITY OF PEACE

CHAPTER 4

THE GOD OF PEACE

Absolute and eternal, God is whole and
undisturbed within himself. Creation at first
reflected that wholeness, that well-being.
Everything was good in and of itself. The
natural world was at rest. Humanity was
at rest. Adam and Eve were at rest within
themselves, with each other, and with God.
CLAUDE RICHARD ALEXANDER JR.,
"BLESSED ARE THE PEACEMAKERS"

God is not nervously pacing the golden streets of heaven, his head held in his hands, muttering, "Oh my *Self*! What am I going to do? I didn't anticipate that people would be debating human sexuality and gender! Quick, Peter, find my book on human ontology! I didn't foresee pandemics. And how was I supposed to know that partisan politics would be driven by brutal social discourse? No one up here could have predicted the rapid rise and ever-present nature of technology. Paul, see if you can set up a Zoom meeting with Bill Gates, Mark Zuckerberg, Jeff Bezos, and Elon Musk. I want to know what the H-E-double hockey sticks is going on down there!"

God sees the whole of human life. He knows a thing or two about health care, marriage, immigration, race relations, education, creation care, fair elections, and just governance. He gets it. He is at peace. He is the God *of* peace. Peace is a core descriptor of God. Our peace has only one source—namely, God's peace. His kind of peace allows us to participate in all human drama as peaceful agents of healing and justice. The God of peace is at work in the world. He will work in you if you would like him to, if you won't be troubled by the change his peace will bring. To receive God's peace requires that we open ourselves to God's renovation of our whole heart, mind, soul, emotions, will, and spirit. His peace operates in us by the Holy Spirit and becomes part of our character, equipping us to take our place in our various areas of human endeavor.

Reaching for God

The Bible proclaims that God "is not far from any one of us. 'For in him we live and move and have our being'" (Acts 17:27–28). Why then is life in God and its corresponding peace so keenly desired but so frustratingly elusive? Are there practices for receiving the God of peace and the peace of God? Yes, let's think a bit about God and us—and how we relate to God.

God is wholly other. He is holy. We know that our sins make us unholy. Our sin cannot abide in his presence. That much most of us know. But too often such knowledge puts us on an treadmill of anxiety as we strive to be good enough so God will want to be near us, consider our thoughts, and hear our prayers. How would your imagination for your relationship with the God of peace change if you were to consider this:

"You are already clean because of the word I have spoken to you. Remain in me, as I also remain in you. No branch can bear fruit by itself; it must remain in the vine. Neither can you bear fruit unless you remain in me.

"I am the vine; you are the branches. If you remain in me and I in you, you will bear much fruit . . .

"As the Father has loved me, so have I loved you. Now remain in my love. If you keep my commands, you will remain in my love, just as I have kept my Father's commands and remain in his love."

JOHN 15:3–5, 9–10

This passage deserves a book of its own. Union with Jesus—like a branch in a vine—is core to Christian spirituality. It is essential to having peace and being a person of peace. Let's observe a few of Jesus' thoughts.

1. **You are already clean.** This saying does not imply that we are perfect or that there will never be other seasons of pruning or spiritual washings. But for our purposes here—for finding and living in peace—it means this: *there is nothing more you need to do to clean yourself up in order to make God like you or want to be with you.* All the cleansing we need was accomplished in the death, burial, and resurrection of Jesus. But we put our judgments of ourselves onto God. We don't like ourselves. A lot of other people don't like us. We assume God, especially a *holy* God, must not want much to do with us either.

We cannot grow in peace if this pattern of thought dominates our relationship with God. Through the words "you are clean," Jesus meant to assure his first followers that their discipleship to him, their hearing and obeying his teachings, meant they were already pruned of wrong ideas about God and his purposes in humanity, in Israel, in the church. What they heard Jesus teach, what they observed in his redemptive deeds of power, what they experienced in his manner of being—even through an arrest, unfair trials, and a brutal, bloody death on a cross awaited Jesus—had brought them into alignment with the purposes of God. Being students of Jesus in kingdom living purified their hearts when it came to love and service to others. The desire and the ability to love God, neighbor, and enemy and to bear the fruit of healing and justice were theirs through abiding in Jesus. Abiding in what God has done, not striving to get him to like us, yields the posture and practice of peace.

2. **You are already loved.** Can this be right—we are loved by Jesus the way his Father loved him? The Father loved Jesus with a love that was *deep*, meaning it went beyond the mere surface issues of life, extending to realities that cannot be contained in space and time. It was *pure* in that it was not contaminated by the human tensions that make untainted love difficult for us. It was *eternal*, which means it existed before Jesus came to this earth as an infant, and thus was not based on performance, on "what Jesus was doing for God." Finally, God's love for Jesus was *perfect*, in that it included all the elements—the various qualities and necessary characteristics for one to feel fully embraced and cared for and valued.

Jesus loves us with that kind of love. The invitation here is to make Jesus' love for you the atmosphere and overall context of your life, not the things of earth. As a branch, you find your true home in the Vine. There is no other source for human meaning and fulfillment. Your home is not found in the things of earth. Thus, the vision for life that comes from being loved by Jesus means that his love for us is what we are most conscious of.

We don't deny daily reality; we inhabit it. But we do so apart from any quest to find love and acceptance—which is maybe the biggest peace stealer of all. Before we enter any moment of life, the love and acceptance of Jesus are already the place where we dwell. Jesus' love is meant to be the place where our hearts and souls are most at rest. It is where we are comfortable enough to get a cold drink from the fridge or prepare a hot cup of tea and put our feet up.

We are most at home when wrapped in love. We are most anxious, even abandoned, when feeling unloved. Most of us routinely go in cycles from being "settled in love" to searching restlessly for something more or better, something that can define us. The story that defines you is one of *already being loved*.

Trinitarian love is more core to your DNA than skin pigment, eye color, IQ, or size. The quality of your being is not defined by the strength, health, or stature of your body. You don't bring the love of God into those things as if they are determinative; you bring them into the reality of God's love and make meaning of them in that way. You are defined by the quality of love you have from Jesus. The fact that we are loved with the same kind of love the Father has for the Son is stunning in the extreme and thus challenging to grasp. We all should spend the rest of our lives coming to experientially know such love. In that love, we will find peace with God, peace within, and peace with others.

3. Remain in Jesus' love. Having told us that we are loved, Jesus invites us to *remain* in that love. This is an invitation to a life in which we *stay put*; we don't roam the earth looking for some thing or some person to make us feel accepted or loved. We simply *abide*; we continue in the place of being loved by God. Thus, love is what gives our life a sense of permanency, a settled state of being. I am loved; therefore I am. I am chosen; therefore I am. I am yoked with Jesus; therefore I am. I am an always existing being with a never-dying future in the new heaven and the new earth; therefore I am!

The classic way to remain in God's love is through the exercise of spiritual practices. These practices don't earn anything—how could they? We are already clean and already loved! Spiritual practices, such as prayer, study, fasting, silence, solitude, and

service to others, are simply the things we do to notice and receive
that which is already real and in place, already accomplished for
us.[1] But what God has done does not set us aside or render us
unresponsive. Engaging in spiritual practices enables an experience of what God has already done and is already doing. When
we use spiritual disciplines, we are not creating something new
that is outside the love of God in Christ. As branches, by the
power of the Holy Spirit, we are simply perceiving and experiencing the life of the Vine, a life made distinct by Trinitarian love.

Paul knew how crucial the experience of the love of God is
to Christian spirituality. It is certainly the only basis for a peace-
filled, peace-multiplying life:

> And I pray that you, being rooted and established in love,
> may have power, together with all the Lord's holy people, to
> grasp how wide and long and high and deep is the love of
> Christ, and to know this love that surpasses knowledge—that
> you may be filled to the measure of all the fullness of God.
>
> Ephesians 3:17–19

Peace is established and grows from the roots of love.
Grasping the truth that we are loved as the Father loved the Son
is our path to peace. Being filled to the measure of all the fullness
of God guarantees that peace will well up in us and overflow to
the people and events in our lives.

Union with God

Peace is found through union with the God of peace. Such union
is described in the phrases "in Christ" or "Christ in you." Those
phrases are used many times in the New Testament. Union with
Christ is clearly a core dimension of Christian life.

This union is far more defining than any personality or

behavior indicator—the Myers-Briggs Type Indicator (MBTI), the DiSC profile, the CliftonStrengths assessment tool, or the Enneagram. To be *in Christ* points to the same reality we referred to earlier when we spoke of *remaining* in Jesus' love. *In Christ* describes a stable state of being, one that is not determined by circumstances. We are *in* Christ, no matter our particular life context. This union means the peace Jesus experienced in his life is available to us.

Though we continue to commit sins, sin is not where we live. Though we are on earth, we are not *in* the world in the sense of being indifferent to or in rebellion against God. We are not in the past, with its mistakes, regrets, or even exploits. We are not in the future, with its fears or hoped-for successes. None of those things define us. If we try to let them define us, we invite anxiety and conflict. If we seek to discover our union with God, little by little we will receive peace and take on the characteristics of a person of peace.

How did the phrase "true identity" come about? You can now find consultants, coaches, psychologists, and personality tests all aimed at helping you discover your "true self." Those resources came into being because there's a large market for them. Apparently, a lot of us don't understand ourselves or don't know who we really are. As a result, a large number of people are needing to invent a self, create an identity. and then try to live consistently with what they create. This work is exhausting. And it creates anxiety.

It is something entirely different to discover and cultivate an identity in Christ. Focusing on that identity relaxes rather than exhausts. Identity in Christ is peaceful, nonanxious. It frees us from using people for their approval.

I know some may protest at this point, "But such a union and the peace one would expect to flow from it—that's not my experience!" Yes, I get it. Replacing anxiety with peace has been a lifelong battle for me too. But what will you choose to be your fundamental guide—your uneven experiences or the facts that you are loved by Jesus the way his Father loved him and are created for union with God?

Can you choose the path of union? Can you let go of discouragement and cynicism? Would you consider it good news to hear that the journey to peace may be less about striving and more about letting go, about opening yourself up to aspects of God that have eluded you? Peace is in God. So don't fixate on examining yourself. Pivot to the *Source*. Gaze on God—especially God in Christ. Receive the Spirit—the fruit of the Spirit.

Yes, God is the Wholly Other. We are not him. But he created us in his image to be in union with him. That reality is baked into the world he designed and created. The world as we know it came from relationship, from a Trinity of beings whose essential character is revealed in so much love, wisdom, and power that we can drop our need to regulate everything in our daily existence and live in peace.

We are created primarily for union. The separation we feel from God is not natural. Jesus came to reveal what is real, to reconcile us to God, and to heal what is broken. This is why Christian spirituality is full of this sentiment:

> Truly my soul finds rest in God;
>   my salvation comes from him.
> Truly he is my rock and my salvation;
>   he is my fortress, I will never be shaken.
>
> PSALM 62:1–2

> "I pray . . . that all of them may be one, Father, just as you are in me and I am in you."
>
> JOHN 17:20–21

> "In him we live and move and have our being."
>
> ACTS 17:28

A Great Mystery

There is a great mystery to this union: God is largely hidden. But his hiddenness does not make union impossible. *Hidden* does not mean absent. The sense that God is absent, writes Martin Laird, a professor of historical theology, "is the great illusion that we are caught up in; it is the human condition."[2] This misconception leads to all manner of anxiety: God is not with me; God doesn't seem to care about my situation; God doesn't hear me; I must have somehow offended God, and now he won't speak to me. These anxious thoughts cannot facilitate peace with God, peace within, and peace in and for the world.

The presence of God is what leads to peace. But presence can be hidden. With babies this is a fun game. We cover our faces with our hands and then pull them away with a "peekaboo!" The baby giggles and along the way learns *object permanence*—grasping that objects or persons continue to exist when they cannot be observed, touched, smelled, or sensed in any way.

But God does not hide from us as if we're playing a game. He is not teasing us. Rather, if God were not largely hidden, he would overwhelm us. He would be too much to take in. We would feel we had no choice in the matter of dealing with him, of loving him or not, of trusting him. No one would be able to avert their eyes or close their ears. Fully revealed, God would be more blinding than the sun and louder than a space shuttle launch. Thus, cultivating object permanence in the spiritual life leads to peace. It means we can be at peace in the middle of profound human difficulty, knowing that God, while perhaps not seen, is there. He is present in the situation, in others, in me.

The wind may blow and toss around the branches that are connected to the Vine. Heavy rain or even hail may buffet them. Harsh sunrays may parch them. But the branches are not those things; those things are just weather.[3] We are in Christ. God's purposes in us, no matter what the barometer or thermometer may say, are more determinative than the passing weather of human life. He is our peace. We are shot through with the DNA of the Vine—even though it is hidden.

Heaven, which is your destiny, has already begun. Jesus is triumphant. Rest peacefully in his victory. You don't have to prove anything, be right about everything, and control the people you love. Someone Else has already proven himself in his Son. He is right about all things. He is in control. Cultivate presence. Learn to see the hidden God at work in the small things, the routines of your daily life. Get out of your thinking head and into heart communion with God. Using only our minds in spirituality makes God seem remote, distant, and outside of us. Communing with God through our hearts brings him and his attributes close. We learn a truism along the line of Augustine: "You were within me, and I was outside myself."[4]

God made peace with us through Jesus' blood shed on the cross, and he is in the process of reuniting all things to their Creator and his creative intention (Colossians 1:20). Peace is present because of God's own presence and his favor toward his people.[5] Peace begins from within in an assurance given by God and extends outward from this center.[6] After the fall, peace has not been an inbuilt characteristic in humanity. It comes and remains as a gift of God. Receive the gift. Give the gift. Take the peace of God, and take your place as a peacemaker.

The God of peace is in the process of saturating earth with his kingdom—his personal and vibrant reign. Central to God's kingdom is peace. We now turn toward discovering the kingdom of peace and exploring how to live peaceful lives within it.

Peace with God: "You are already clean." Ponder these words. Let down your guard; let this truth draw you close to God. Maybe God isn't looking at you in anger, wanting to clean you up. Maybe you are loved right where you are and are now extended an invitation to be with and to follow Jesus. Deeply consider this proposition, and say yes to any invitation you hear from the Spirit.

Peace Within: Maybe you are the angry one who belittles yourself for an inability to get rid of certain patterns of sin. Can you cease *anxious reaching* and peacefully accept union with God? Consider ways you can do that.

Peace for the Sake of the World: How can you become a person of peace, such that you are a well of peace from which others drink? What new attitudes, practices, and relational norms do you need to adopt? Pick one and gently begin in a spirit of hopefulness. Notice what is different about you, and be mindful of the way others respond to you.

CHAPTER 5

THE PEACE OF GOD'S KINGDOM

This is my Father's world . . .
I rest me in the thought . . .
That though the wrong seems oft so strong,
God is the Ruler yet.
    MALTBIE DAVENPORT BABCOCK, "THIS IS
    MY FATHER'S WORLD" (EMPHASIS MINE)

I hate high-rise hotels. This is true, even though they usually have nice lobbies, well-appointed meeting rooms, good restaurants and large, and pleasantly decorated rooms. So what's the problem? Elevators—jam-packed elevators every morning and evening. They drive me nuts! My breathing gets really shallow. Cologne, sweat, and cigarette odor choke me to the point of gagging. And what if something happens to the elevator? I have a friend in the elevator business who has assured me a few times that the odds of getting stuck on an elevator are very low. But then I read a news story about people stuck in an elevator. I know then that I am right and my friend is wrong! In one way or another, the vast majority of us feel trapped or suffocated by some element of life.

It appears we are all trapped by and being manipulated by a wicked algorithm.[1] Huge tech corporations dictate human life and dominate the stock market. Even if we wanted to protest and flee, we can't because too many of us and our loved ones have investment and retirement funds that are dominated by tech stocks. From a political point of view, we are trapped in the dysfunction of a two-party system—with each side teaching their adherents to hate the opposite side. Some of us feel entombed by racial or gender prejudice. Others feel stuck in an inescapable financial rut. Brutal tyrants carry out their evil around the world. They deceive and snare people with their egotistical ruthlessness. Immigrants, desperately fleeing atrocious human conditions, face grim obstacles—horror on one side, rejection on the other.

Just typing these words makes my mental claustrophobia act up! When we imagine that evil kingdoms are in charge of the world, our hearts shudder and our guts twist into knots. Feeling trapped leads to hasty, aggressive jerks and twists, and we often make big mistakes as we try to do anything possible to escape. The accompanying anxiety is unhealthy for our soul and for those around us.

The reality of being twisted into knots affects others. *The nature we create within us nurtures the atmosphere around us.* Consider these questions: What makes me lose my peace? What kind of person do I want to be? What kind of legacy do I want to leave in my sphere of influence? What subconscious rationales do I find myself creating such that I would betray my legacy goals in order to engage in peaceless behaviors? It is these subconscious motivations that we, as apprentices to Jesus, need to work on. These internal processes create our *heart*. Jesus always focused on the heart and on that which shapes it:

Jesus called the crowd to him and said, "Listen and understand. What goes into someone's mouth does not defile them, but what comes out of their mouth, that is what defiles them . . .

"Are you still so dull?" Jesus asked them. "Don't you see that whatever enters the mouth goes into the stomach and then out of the body? But the things that come out of a person's mouth *come from the heart*, and these defile them. For *out of the heart* come evil thoughts—murder, adultery, sexual immorality, theft, false testimony, slander. These are what defile a person; but eating with unwashed hands does not defile them."

MATTHEW 15:10–11, 16–20 (EMPHASIS MINE)

Having peace and extending peace among the people and events of one's life are matters of one's heart. What comprises a heart at peace and one that lives in peace with others? *It is a heart oriented toward and animated and energized by the kingdom of God.* Jesus oriented his ministry around the kingdom of God. He taught about it, demonstrated it in deeds of power, and modeled it in his way of being in the world. Though the kingdom is central to Jesus' teaching, Christians don't always clearly understand what it means.

Kingdom means "rule" or "reign." Think of it as a realm or a sphere of influence. When we say "the kingdom of God," we are describing the sphere of God's ultimate, determinative power—his rule or reign. Thus, the kingdom of God is present in all the places in which what God wills is, in fact, the reality. This is why Jesus taught us to pray, "Your kingdom come, your will be done, on earth as it is in heaven" (Matthew 6:10). This prayer does several important things: it increases our appetite for the reign of God in our lives, aligns our will with the will of God, and shapes our words and deeds toward the goodness of the kingdom, toward being ourselves an answer to the prayer.

The inbreaking of God's kingdom was a pivotal and decisive moment. Jesus came onto the human scene, declaring that the whole story of the world was being completed in him. He described this dramatic intervention in terms of the reign of God as a present, interactive aspect of human life. He then asked his hearers to repent, to reconsider their whole lives—their plans, hopes, goals, and dreams; their approach to religion, worldview, and politics—in light of his announcement. He asked his hearers to believe—to place their confidence for living—in him and in his good news.

This is the way Mark's gospel records Jesus' explosion into human history: "Jesus went into Galilee, proclaiming the good news of God. 'The time has come,' he said. 'The kingdom of God has come near. Repent and believe the good news!'" (Mark 1:14–15).

The Everyday and Ordinary

Finding our truest life within the kingdom Jesus described is the core context for feeling grounded, safe, and secure in this world. If we don't live in the kingdom and derive power for our daily lives from it, we are relegated to being oppressed by bad religion, deceived into adopting false worldviews, unsettled by the ups and downs of economies and stock markets, and tossed about by politicians, political parties, and election cycles. Only secure people live consistently in peace. The insecure are too busy using the people and events in their lives to secure themselves, to find safety. Doing so kills peace within and allows only anxiety and fear to spill over into our words and deeds, which in turn destroys any chance of being a peacemaker in the world.

Jesus was a peacemaker because he did not have to run from human predicaments. He was not tainted by them; rather, he brought reality to them. Peace can feel buried under alarming news stories or hurtful conversations that unnerve us. We want to work toward the ability to be in a painful reality but not be fully colored by it. Peace can a part of the hue, the tone, the shade of any tough setting.

Life in the kingdom is not an ideal or merely a future hope for heaven. In his instructions to the church in Rome about the concrete context of authentic spirituality, the apostle Paul wrote:

> Take your everyday, ordinary life—your sleeping, eating, going-to-work, and walking-around life—and place it before God as an offering. Embracing what God does for you is the best thing you can do for him. Don't become so well-adjusted to your culture that you fit into it without even thinking. Instead, fix your attention on God. You'll be changed from the inside out. Readily recognize what he wants from you, and quickly respond to it. Unlike the culture around you, always dragging you down to its level of immaturity, God brings the best out of you, develops well-formed maturity in you.
>
> ROMANS 12:1–2 MSG

The everyday and ordinary is the realm where God rules, where peace is experienced, and where peacemakers do their work. Peace is not primarily personal piety; peace is a lived, public reality. We cultivate peace, and then we offer ourselves to God as peacemakers within the calendar events and relationships of daily living.

Fixating on the fleeting moments of what passes for news sends us spiraling down a hole of anxiety, fear, distress, quarreling, and conflict. Think of it this way: *we are in the news, but the news does not have to be in us.* The news does not define us, lead us, or shape us. Having made peace with God, having made

God's purposes the vision of our life, we take our place in the news of the day as nonanxious people who are alert to the Spirit who mediates to us the reign of God. The Spirit, in turn, guides us, as his cooperative friends, into the things that make for peace.

The story of God can be summarized in this way:

- the creation of the first humans and their invitation to colabor with God
- the calling of Abraham and the creation of Israel as the people through whom God would save the world
- the creation of the church through the coming of Jesus and the sending of the Spirit

This is the story of a people oriented to their Maker and his calling on their lives and to those they are meant to serve. The revelation of God is meant to be discerned in the people and activities of your life. The potential to be a servant of God to others is there as well. We may think, *Yes, but trouble is there too!* Of course it is. But what is *trouble* in the midst of the kingdom— the reality of knowing that God has the ultimate rule over human affairs?

Life within the absolute dominion of God's kingdom is peace; life in the world of scarcity is conflict, an aggressive and hostile fighting for one's piece of the pie. Life in the kingdom of God as a follower of Jesus is security and confidence; life in the kingdom of the world is insecurity, anxiety, uncertainty, and self-doubt. People alive in the kingdom make peace; the walking dead of the world make trouble.

The inbreaking of the kingdom means we are never alone, never sealed off from God. As we turn to the next section of this chapter, we'll work together to discern a crucial truth that leads to a life of peace: *God is always already present.*

God Is Always Already Present

Peace is dependent on a deep, experiential knowledge of the biblical promise made by God: "I will be with you." As the prophet Isaiah declared, "'Though the mountains be shaken and the hills be removed, yet my unfailing love for you will not be shaken nor my covenant of peace be removed,' says the LORD, who has compassion on *you*" (Isaiah 54:10, emphasis mine).

Consciously or subconsciously, the fear that God is far away, absent, doing something more important than paying attention to me, or that he is so mad at me he won't even look at me, fills the imagination of peace-challenged followers of Jesus. Our actual understanding of God the Father—not what we think we *should* believe—is a reliable indicator of our ability to live in peace and pass it on to others.

As I write, the world is in a mess. We are still in the grips of a pandemic, economic collapse, angry political division, racial tension, and a growing mental health crisis. Has God finally become totally fed up and is leaving us to our own devices so we will spiral down even further into human brokenness and corruption? Where is God when things are going wrong and a turnaround point is not in view? How we answer this question in the most honest part of our heart will determine the degree of our peace with God and of our peace within, as well as the extent of our ability to be a peacemaker in the world. Feeling abandoned does not make for peace, while feeling cherished by God brings great peace.

An important mental image for peaceful living is the fact that *humanity remains God's project*. This must mean that God stays close to his broken creation. He is not an absentee owner. Personal presence is his managerial style. Finding peace means coming to the deep, experiential knowledge of the many Scriptures that express a fundamental biblical promise of God: "I will be with you."

In contrast, various forms of fear shout, "That is not true. God is not with me!" If hard times or challenging circumstances come, ones in which there is no intuitive, quick way out, it must mean God is distant or ignorant of my situation or incapable of doing anything about it. Such fear is a prime peace robber.

But what if the actual state of all reality is, in the words of Dallas Willard, "a community of boundless and totally competent love"?[2] Could the community of Trinity ever be noncommunal, nonrelational—kicking its image bearers to the curb? Does boundless love have limits if things get too challenging, too broken, too sinful among humans? Can total competence be limited by the global complexities of the twenty-first century?

Again, how we sincerely answer these questions is a reliable predictor of having either peace or anxiety about our essential safety in the world. The Scriptures insist on a vision, a view of the world that naturally produces peace within and peace in relationships. Consider these examples.

1. At the death of Moses, Joshua is told he will assume Moses's role as leader of God's people and will guide them into the Promised Land. Such an assignment would produce anxiety in anyone. God knows this about his creation. Joshua hears God say to him, "Have I not commanded you? Be strong and courageous. Do not be afraid; do not be discouraged, for the LORD your God will be with you wherever you go" (Joshua 1:9). The presence of God is the promise. Presence produces peace in moments of panic. This truth alerts us to a key to spirituality in the way of Jesus: *learn to practice the presence of God in your day-to-day life.*

2. When Israel was exiled in Babylon, with no knowledge of if or when deliverance would come, perhaps wondering if God had banished them from himself forever, Isaiah

strengthened the people of God with these words: "So do not fear, for I am with you; do not be dismayed, for I am your God. I will strengthen you and help you; I will uphold you with my righteous right hand" (Isaiah 41:10). Again, the vehicle for peace is *withness*. It is relationship—"for I am your God." This *withness* is a strength, a help, a solid place to stand in the fearful, confusing moments of life.

3. When Paul taught the church in Rome, he explained basic principles associated with following Jesus. Peace-challenged people have nurtured themselves with these words for twenty centuries: "I am convinced that neither death nor life, neither angels nor demons, neither the present nor the future, nor any powers, neither height nor depth, nor anything else in all creation, will be able to separate us from the love of God that is in Christ Jesus our Lord" (Romans 8:38–39). When Jesus is your Lord, nothing can separate you from God's love. Nothing broken inside you. No circumstance engulfing you. Nothing in the past or in the future. Nothing near, nothing far. Nothing seen or unseen.

The promise is *love*. Being cared for, as love does. Experiencing peace, as being loved and cared for allow. You may feel stigmatized by church, denounced by family, and excluded from social circles, but wherever you are, you are not out of the reach of the love of God in Jesus.

True, but Livable?

We appreciate those Bible passages, but in daily living they often seem far from us. Does it mean we hold these ideas to be *true* but *distant* from us or *unlivable*? Making the Bible's vision for peace a reality in our lives is a matter of focus, of being alert to and noticing the person and work of God always with us. During the past couple of decades, I've found great help for noticing God through Ignatian spirituality. Ignatius of Loyola was a gravely wounded soldier who found fervent faith in God. He put rhythms and practices into his life to help him know and love God more and follow Jesus more closely. He became well known for helping others do the same.

Ignatian spirituality is best known for "its insistence that God is at work everywhere—in work, relationships, culture, the arts, the intellectual life, creation itself. As Ignatius put it, all the things in the world are presented to us 'so that we can know God more easily and make a return of love more readily.'"[3] Ignatian practices teach us that a proper spiritual life "focuses on God at work *now*. It fosters an active attentiveness to God joined with a prompt responsiveness to God. God calls; we respond."[4] Ignatius teaches us to notice God at work in our feelings and our desires—our hearts.

The spirituality of Ignatius helps us pursue interior freedom. Ignatius teaches that we should seek "to be free of personal preferences, superfluous attachments, and preformed opinions . . . Ignatius counseled radical detachment: 'We should not fix our desires on health or sickness, wealth or poverty, success or failure, a long life or a short one.' Our one goal is the freedom to make a wholehearted choice to follow God."[5] This approach is commonly called "Ignatian indifference." Not indifference in the sense that I don't care about anything, but indifference in that all my desires and preferences are made second to loving and following Jesus and serving others.

For me, the most helpful, peace-promoting aspect of Ignatian spirituality is the practice of *examen*—a review of the day's activities with an eye to detecting and responding to the presence of God.[6] Sometimes I'll go over my day just by memory; other times I use the calendar on my phone, noticing where I found *consolation*—high points wherein I noticed God and interacted with him—or *desolation*—low points wherein I was unaware of God's active presence, which may have led to fear, anxiety, and doubt.[7] As I review my day with God, I try to be alert to moments of peace and anxiety, grace and judgment, Spirit power and fleshly weakness.

In the last few years, I have found what is for me the most fruitful pattern for practicing the company of God. It is a three-part rhythm: dedication, presence, and examen.

I begin the day with *dedication*—committing myself and the events and people of my day to God. I use various prayers and readings that assist me in consecrating and surrendering my life, my relationships, and my work to God.

Throughout the day I recite to myself little phrases that bring me back to noticing the *presence* of God and keep me grounded in the present moment:

- Come, Holy Spirit; give me the gifts I need for this moment.
- Come, Great Shepherd. (I often recite Psalm 23.)
- Come, reign of God. (Your kingdom come, your will be done.)
- I am always safe in the kingdom of God.
- Help me be a gracious, generous, generative person in this moment.
- May the words of my mouth, the meditations of my heart, and the thoughts of my mind be pleasing to you, O God.

At night I practice *examen*—reviewing my day in gratitude, learning what I can about God, myself, and others.

Dedication, presence, examen—these are three strong practices for finding peace. With God, as we've come to notice, being always already on the scene, we don't have to strive to get our own way at the expense of others, at the expense of peace. This three-part rhythm has not just enhanced peace; it has focused and slowed my life, further enabling me to notice that God is always already in the midst of my life.

In the next chapter, I'll touch on some common barriers and bridges to choosing peace with God.

Peace with God: Peace with God is not an idea or concept. It is relational and is experienced through the presence of God. Recall times when you felt the close presence of God. Feel the peace—and the grounded security and hope that come with peace. Let these memories stir in you an increased longing for the presence of God.

Peace Within: If God is always already in your world, you don't have to make things happen. Consider times when your inner being has shouted, *That is not true!* Examine those occasions with the goal of bringing your whole self into sincere confidence that the world you inhabit is the realm of "a community of boundless and totally competent love." Can you feel the peace this reality brings?

Peace for the Sake of the World: You are called *by* God, *to* Jesus, *for* the sake of the world. The kingdom is at work in the world, and the ultimate end of the world is assured. Yet the world is scary. Adopt the following words as your commissioning for life: "Be strong and courageous. Fear not. I am with you." Visualize the reality that you are always safe in God's kingdom. Imagine how this truth arms you to be both at peace and a peacemaker.

CHAPTER 6

CHOOSING PEACE WITH GOD

> *We are not at peace with others because we*
> *are not at peace with ourselves, and we are not*
> *at peace with ourselves because we are not at*
> *peace with God.*
>
> THOMAS MERTON, *THE LIVING BREAD*

We seek peace in a variety of ways before finding peace with God.

Lucas's college roommate, Baker, was driving along the river to his part-time job when he died in an accident late in the spring of their sophomore year, just before classes were to end for the summer. After an emotional summer in which every routine brought the loss of Baker to Lucas's mind, fall approached, bringing with it the first day of school. Lucas wasn't sure he could face it. He was afraid that every hallway and room would carry memories he would rather keep stuffed. As he pushed away the memories, he became aware that he was also stuffing the grim feelings attached to the memories.

Without realizing it, stress and anxiety were leaking into his soul. Trying to be helpful, his friends suggested he seek some peace through yoga. He went to a few classes, but they didn't seem to touch the depths of his soul.

* * *

Worried about her increasing anxiety, Mia tried meditation. It helped a bit, but she couldn't find the motivation to have a consistent practice, so she said yes to an invitation to try a friend's church. *Spirituality* sounded to her like it must include big helpings of peace. But it didn't take Mia long to figure out that church isn't always spiritual, and that some spiritualities are driven by fear and fueled by anger, not peace. Early in her church journey, she found she had a question. She was confused and hurt to discover that apparently having questions meant she wasn't a real Christian. When she told her small group leader, Jess, that she didn't understand how an ancient series of writings—the Bible—could be authoritative in a scientific age, she unknowingly pushed all the buttons of fear and anger inside Jess. To Jess, Mia's comments were a clear example that in modern culture, biblical reliability was being stolen out from underneath him. He was angry that people did not respect the core of his religion. The tragedy is that Mia wasn't asking the question because she thought the Bible had no authority; she assumed it did. She just didn't understand how and why. Mia walked out of church sad that the peace she was seeking wasn't to be found there.

These stories, and many others like them, alert us to a vital insight about seeking peace: a peaceful life comes through peace with God. No matter how sincere our intentions may be, peace that does not begin with and find its deepest source in peace with God is a false, temporary, or feigned peace.

Seeking peace means making a simple but stark decision: Do you want to make God and his plan the center of your life? If you do, something surprising will happen: the things you now think of as central—career, family, hobbies, vacations, consumer goods—will become more meaningful and stewarded better with God at the center of your life.

After miraculously feeding five thousand people with five loaves of bread and two fish (John 6:1–15), Jesus described what should be at the center of one's life. A large crowd, astonished at the inexplicable demonstration of Jesus' power over the material world, went looking for him. Jesus knew they were missing the point. The crowd may have had some spiritual curiosity, but mostly they were seeking food. But for Jesus, food was only an analogy. He was teaching the disciples a crucial underlying truth about the source of peace: they never needed to fear in moments of scarcity, in times when life was hard, confusing, or painful.

Like those throngs of hungry people, we often find our lives filled with some sort of *lack*, which then produces feelings of impotence and fear. Jesus wanted his apprentices to move beyond the constant fear of scarcity. He desired for them to know that the little they assumed themselves to have—little spirituality, little understanding of the things Jesus taught, little love for each other, for neighbor, or for enemy—when blessed by Jesus would always be more than enough. There would be an abundance. When God is *enough* on your behalf, you are at peace.

Jesus, ever the master teacher, shared with his disciples the real point: "Do not work for the food that perishes, but for the food that endures to eternal life, which the Son of Man will give to you" (John 6:27 ESV). Rather, said Jesus, "The work of God is this: to believe in the one he has sent" (John 6:29). The point Jesus wanted to drive home: "I am the bread of life. Whoever comes to me will never go hungry, and whoever believes in me will never be thirsty" (John 6:35).

Let's take these teachings of Jesus one at a time.

Food That Perishes

The crowd had spent a lot of creative energy figuring out where Jesus was and then making their way to him. They were striving for bread that over time would mold, and for fish that before long would stink. Bread and fish perish. Jesus said we shouldn't spend our lives on those things (John 6:27). To find peace with God, you must honestly answer a question: Does Jesus know what he's talking about? Do I believe he is right? If you're not inclined to have confidence in what Jesus says and therefore you strive for things that depreciate as the central or animating factor of your life, you will soon find yourself trapped and craving freedom.

Here is the first step: don't merely struggle to say no to current desires—though you may have to do so for a "training period." Fundamentally, you want to cultivate a new set of desires that more or less automatically set aside disordered desires in favor of seeking things that have the fragrance of eternity to them. It works like this: we cultivate the desire to love and serve the opposite sex. This naturally eliminates them from being merely objects of some sort of pleasure. We cultivate the desire for our lives to be for the good of others, which overrides the urge to use people for our gain. We cultivate a desire for love, which in turn rules out hatred and harm.

The *Work* of God Is to *Believe*

The term *work* in John 6:29 does not refer to what Christians rightly fear—namely, working to earn salvation or favor from

God. Here *work* refers to that which cooperates with what God wants, what he requires or expects from his chosen people, his cooperative friends. *Work* indicates *obedience*. But not in a weird, stilted, religious way. What is in view here is a joyful, active obedience that arises from respect for God and his intention for humanity.

You'll get the picture if you think of the respect and the "desire to be like you" that a young baseball player might have for Mike Trout or an aspiring musician might have for Adele or Usher, or the way an aspiring civic leader might look up to Kamala Harris or Marco Rubio. In these cases, the student is saying to the master, "I respect what you do and how you do it—even the person you are. I want to be like you. Therefore I will obediently take batting tips or vocal lessons from you." Jesus wants something similar from his followers.

Jesus said this work is "to believe." What exactly did Jesus have in mind here? The Amplified Bible helps us get at it: "This is the work of God: that you believe [adhere to, trust in, rely on, and have faith] in the One whom He has sent" (John 6:29 AMP).

This *work of belief* is a simple, cooperative response to God's initiative. Note that Jesus did not say there is nothing to do whatsoever. The spiritual life does require effort, but such effort is never done to impress God. God is already so impressed with you that he gave his one and only Son in order to have you as his cooperative son or daughter for all of eternity. Thus, the work in view here comes from a childlike but passionate yearning to be with God, to do what he is doing, on his terms and in his way. Have that yearning in your heart, and you will surely have peace with God.

Moving past mere belief *in* Jesus to actually trusting him and relying on his worldview, and then arranging the affairs of our lives accordingly, is a crucial move for people who are seeking peace. Mere belief *about* Jesus is not enough. We must believe *him* as we would our trusted parents or friends. Without this deep belief, profound peace is not possible. We will remain unsettled in our souls and likely become persons who, rather than radiating peace to others, exude a troubled and troubling presence.

The Problem of God

Seeking fulfillment in Jesus does raise a problem. God can be an inconvenient truth. Do you really want there to be *a way that things are* according to an intelligent creator? Do you really want to pursue the submission and alignment that such a notion calls for? What if doing so were to impinge on human sexuality? On global commerce? On race relations and other ways we treat one another? On whether there is such a thing as *truth*? Be honest. Peace hangs in the balance.

Is peace something you seek like a lover of old cars who searches the ancient barns of America, like an investor seeking the highest-yielding deal? Do you find it natural to "seek first [God's] kingdom" (Matthew 6:33)? When the things of the kingdom are real within us, peace will be as well—enough peace to share. The great irony is that the perceived problem—namely, God—is the source, conveyor, and eternal insurer of peace.

Peace isn't just an aspect of God's being; it is a key plotline throughout his story. God, out of his peaceful essence, created in peace. It was not a big, sweaty strain. And whatever else may surprise us about eternity, we can know for sure that God's new reality will be saturated in perfect peace. Between those times, peace hangs around in the story like ripe fruit. It is available to those who seek it and pick it. But not all seek it.

Acts 17 recounts the story of Paul's efforts to help the Athenians see what is real. Paul wanted them to see what is unmovable in the best sense of the term—the way unmovable ground is a solid foundation for a home. The people of Athens were tossed about by various religious theories about the gods, about what appeased them, what brought goodness, and what offended them, unleashing their angry judgment on one's life. Paul said, "While God has overlooked the times of human ignorance, now he commands all people everywhere to repent, because he has fixed a day on which he will have the world judged in righteousness by a man whom he has appointed, and of this he has given assurance to all by raising him from the dead" (Acts 17:30–31 NRSV).

Paul's thought runs like this: Jesus rose from the dead, which confirms there is a God who intends certain things in and from his creation. He has appointed a day when his intentions will become realized. He understands that we humans don't always get this, so he calls on us to repent. *Repent* is the English translation of the Greek term *metanoein*. It means "to be mindful of one's life." We might say, "to think back on my life." It is an invitation to analysis: Am I living in the light of and in alignment with the will of God?

If you think about this long enough and with enough honesty, you may confront this question: Do I even *want* to rethink my life? Is there something else, some other path I value more? Repentance has its most profound effect on the truly honest. If you're not sure you want peace with God through discovering his created intentions for you, tell him why. He can handle it. As you talk it out with God, you will be entering the light of God—a light that will illuminate aspects of life you've never seen before. You will be surprised. A joy you have never known will be a cherished by-product of peace with God. You get there through surrender and cooperation, through submission and collaboration.

The Inescapable God

The New Revised Standard Version titles Psalm 139 "The Inescapable God." God is inescapable in that he has a plan for our

lives that is stronger than the humorous caricature of a Jewish
mother! The idea of someone else having a plan for your life can
be a big peace killer. If you wanted to be an artist but your dad
compelled you to follow in his footsteps to medical school, you
know what I mean. If Mom steered you toward math or law while
you yearned for sports medicine or pediatric nursing, you know
how inescapable such expectations can be.

Is God worse than a nagging parent, insisting that he have
his way in us? Why does he get to choose? If he loves me, doesn't
he want me to follow my own path? What about my DNA, my
destiny, or the environment in which I was raised? Are they not
determinative? The psalmist grappled with similar thoughts:

> Where can I go from your spirit?
> Or where can I flee from your presence? . . .
> If I say, "Surely the darkness shall cover me,
> and the light around me become night,"
> even the darkness is not dark to you;
> the night is as bright as the day,
> for darkness is as light to you.
>
> PSALM 139:7, 11–12 NRSV

In Psalm 139 we hear a voice marked by praise, complaint,
and tension. In helping us seek peace with God, I want to high-
light the sentences that seem to convey the way the greatness of
God can feel like a nagging truth. A rough paraphrase might
be, "God, you bug me! I can't hide from you anywhere. You find
me even in the dark." The awareness that God had an up-close,
personal knowledge of David was a lot to take in. I wonder if it
felt oppressive and overbearing? Or freeing and comforting? How
we feel about the inescapable nature of God may well have to do
with our fundamental, underlying desires.

We say we want to be close to God, and that was, of course,

true for David. So why the displeasure about his inability to run to a place where he would be out of God's sight? This is the *problem* of the inescapable God. But once we find peace with God, being in God's presence becomes a *celebration* of fulfilled desire in God. David gives us the vision and the rationale required to stop fighting God and to find peace in him:

> For it was you who formed my inward parts;
>> you knit me together in my mother's womb . . .
> I am fearfully and wonderfully made . . .
>> My frame was not hidden from you,
> when I was being made in secret,
>> intricately woven in the depths of the earth.
> Your eyes beheld my unformed substance.
> In your book were written
>> all the days that were formed for me,
>> when none of them as yet existed.
>
> PSALM 139:13–16 NRSV

Imagine yourself praying, "God, please bring to full flower my Psalm 139 self. I trust your intention more than my confused desires. I want what you want. I want to follow the path you set for me. I want to be the kind of person who can do all the good you created me to do." In so praying we are asking what the Anglican bishop George Appleton asked: "Take me down to the spring of my life, and tell me my nature and my name. Give me freedom to grow, so that I may become that self, the seed of which You planted in me at my making."[1]

At the beginning, these sorts of prayers are like flashes of brilliance. But as we move on in peace with God, they become very natural. As our desires are reshaped and we progress in the repentance Jesus and Paul call for, David's prayer becomes intuitive and gets deeper and more meaningful each time we pray:

Search me, O God, and know my heart;
test me and know my thoughts.
See if there is any wicked way in me,
and lead me in the way everlasting.

PSALM 139:23–24 NRSV

We now have some insight about the God of peace and his will for our lives. In the next section of this chapter, we'll explore how we go about choosing peace with him.

Desiring Peace with God

The Bible encourages us to "submit to God and be at peace with him; in this way prosperity will come to you" (Job 22:21). But submission is daunting. We intuitively fear it will cramp our style. We fear that its outcome will disappoint us.

Jeremiah felt *the problem of God*, and he had to decide if the will of God was a prickly wound or a blessing: "Before I [God] formed you in the womb I knew you, before you were born I set you apart; I appointed you as a prophet to the nations" (Jeremiah 1:5).

When Isaiah was commissioned (Isaiah 6), all he could feel was "woe" over what he perceived to be his and his people's unclean hearts. He didn't think he could fulfill his calling. Noah had the weirdest of all inescapable callings. He had no precedents to rely on, just the crazy command to build a boat that would rescue a remnant of creation from a coming flood. We may picture Abraham (who was called Abram at the time) minding his own business when suddenly the voice on his GPS said, "Recalculating . . . You are now leaving Ur to, uh, well, I'm not sure! Just follow the blue line. I'll give you directions as you go." We can't know for sure what Abram thought and felt about his encounter with the inescapable God. We just know this: "So Abram went" (Genesis 12:4).

Moses, who was full of self-doubt, was seriously reluctant to believe that God was actually calling to him from a burning bush that wasn't being consumed by the fire. Can you blame him? If God were going to talk, wouldn't you imagine something grander—like an earthquake or a lightning bolt?

Women in Bible times would have felt they weren't allowed to be leaders. But God, as we know, can be a persistent problem. Women worthy of admiration, such as Esther, Deborah, Miriam, Huldah, Mary of Bethany, Mary Magdalene, Lydia, Phoebe, Priscilla, and many other women at Pentecost, found their way over long-standing barriers to hear a clear divine call and to follow it. The Twelve and the women with them certainly didn't think, *Well, yes, of course—we can see why Jesus bypassed the religious leaders and chose us simple, uneducated folk!*

Our hearing of the call isn't always consistent. It can bubble up from a deep place within us, but it can also come from an initiative outside of us—no matter what a personality inventory might say. These kinds of callings cause wrestling with God. In that wrestling we find in the end not a problem but our best, most faithful Friend. But to be *chosen* brings *obedience* into the picture. *Chosen* takes us back to the problem of the inescapable God.

The real question is this: Does God measure up to whatever standard you have for someone to whom you would submit yourself? If not, why not? What is your issue, frustration, or accusation regarding God? If you have one, you are not hiding it from him, so you may as well get it out by talking it over with him. He'll be okay, and you will too. You'll be better than okay. Healing and revelation will come, along with fulfillment and peace. But being suspicious of God means we don't trust him as a reliable leader in life, and thus we can have no peace with him.

If that's true for you, the most important thing you can do is talk to God honestly about it. If talking to God feels odd or counterintuitive, ask yourself a few questions: *What is holding me back from talking to God? Do I feel I have something to lose? Am I afraid of something?* God will meet you in your honest reflection.

To choose peace with God requires heartfelt, unfeigned faith in God. While faith is a gift, it functions best with a rationale for it. Such a foundation is found in the story of God.

Finding Peace in the Story of God

Creation was spoken into existence in peace. Through the erratic periods of the patriarchs, judges, kings, and prophets, God's story is implemented in peace. God never lost his peace when the world was going wildly wrong. Peace has been a defining aspect of the entire divine story, and peace will find its fullest expression in the completed story.

Peace in Creation

What do you think God was feeling and experiencing during creation? "I don't know!" you might respond. Of course, none of us could *know* such a thing. But because you have a "God concept," you have an intuition about it. Just stop for a moment and make conscious that which sits every day in your subconscious. Do you imagine that God was uptight, hoping that things would turn out okay and that his spoken commands would have their intended effect—that his "let there be light" would actually *work*? Do you imagine God was fearful in a Frankenstein, Jurassic Park sort of way—anxiously hoping his experiment did not spin out of control?

Of course not. The narrative of Genesis oozes with peace. The image of the Spirit of God hovering over the waters is reminiscent of a tranquil, foggy morning when everything is especially still. "Let there be," followed by "and it was so," has such a strong rhythm that creation is seen as concretely assured. As creation unfurled, each aspect was called good. *Good* means that the unfolding will of God in physical creation was excellent. God was making a habitation that was perfectly suitable for you and me to live in. Do you believe that? Or when you see the imperfections in the world, do you worry about whether you are safe on this planet, in our universe, in the cosmos? Peace with God will come only when you can settle down, like you do in your favorite chair, into the "and it was good" creation of God.

When God finished creating, do you believe he was like a fretful playwright, worried about what the cosmic version of tough New York or London newspaper critics would write about his handiwork? Do you imagine that he was nervous about whether everything would hold together—that gravity would actually keep things in place and bodily systems would actually do their jobs? Of course not. Nor should we have a mental picture of a tired God, acting as though he had just run a marathon or finished a big term paper by pulling an all-nighter.

How do such ideas make any sense, given that God is all-powerful and all-knowing? As the prophets of old said:

> Have you not known? Have you not heard?
> The LORD is the everlasting God,
>   the Creator of the ends of the earth.
> He does not faint or grow weary;
>   his understanding is unsearchable.
>
> ISAIAH 40:28 NRSV

> "Ah, Sovereign LORD, you have made the heavens and the earth by your great power and outstretched arm. Nothing is too hard for you."
>
> JEREMIAH 32:17

God wasn't burned-out and anxious in the process of creation. He simply finished the work of creation and rested. Since then, he has been superintending creation toward the fulfillment of his purposes. In the book of Nehemiah, the Levites explain:

> "You alone are the LORD;
> You have made heaven,
> The heaven of heavens, with all their host,
> The earth and everything on it,
> The seas and all that is in them,
> And You preserve them all."
>
> NEHEMIAH 9:6 NKJV

Rest in the context of creation simply means God ceased. He stopped because he was done. What he imagined, and the future to which it all pointed, was completed. Completion or achievement indicates peacefulness. Something left incomplete carries a sense of anxiousness, unease, unsettledness. With that in mind, an invitation stands open before us: to place our fractured, incomplete, imperfect lives into the competed work of God: "And God said . . . And it was so . . . And God saw that it was good . . . By the seventh day God had finished the work" (Genesis 1:3, 7, 10; 2:2). And as the life of God's one and only Son—a life given for our redemption—was drawing to an end, Jesus, in peace, said, "It is finished" (John 19:30).

Peace in the Fall

We often think, *Well, okay, God made it through creation in peace, but he had to be out-of-control angry that the first humans ruined creation.* I understand why we might think that, but it's highly likely we are projecting our feelings onto God. A favorite story in our family reveals what I have in mind. When our two children were young, our son loved the Star Wars movies. He had almost finished putting together a puzzle depicting a Star Wars scene when his younger sister and friend, not really understanding the pain they were about to cause, tore the puzzle apart. I'm pretty sure our son lost his peace! That, or some scene similar to it, is what we imagine God felt like when the first humans tore perfection apart.

Again, we can't know the true feelings of God, but we can observe his actions and infer his feelings from those. So what did God do when Adam sinned? He made a relational move. He called for Adam: "Where are you?" (Genesis 3:9). God did not want to know, like in a game of hide-and-seek, where Adam was. We've already said that God is all-knowing. God wanted Adam to recognize his condition, to see where he was—namely, hiding from God. Through God's reaction to the perpetrators of the fall, we see that he is always lovingly and peacefully close to his broken creation. He stays near while desiring two things: that we would see the truth of ourselves, and that we would see him for who he is—the world's one true Creator Lord, who loves his creation and stands ready to have a relationship with them, even when they've blown things up.

Peace in the New Heaven and New Earth

The story concerning the God of peace can be briefly summarized: God created humanity for his own wise and loving purposes. Humankind has lived in ways contrary to those purposes. Acting in harmony with who he is by nature, God, through patriarchs, judges, kings, and prophets, stayed with his project in love and peace. The beginning of the final act saw God sending his one and only Son to earth to redeem humanity, to create one new people who would be ambassadors of his kingdom and reign with him forever in the new heaven and new earth (Revelation 22:5).

It is with this in mind that Peter wrote, "In keeping with his [God's] promise, we are looking forward to a new heaven and a new earth, where righteousness dwells" (2 Peter 3:13). As portrayed in the book of Revelation, the scenes in heaven are full of peace. John begins by conveying to his readers the peace of God. Peace is implicit in the second coming of Christ and in the final victory of God. The conflict within the scenes of Revelation find its peaceful resolution in Jesus. The throne in heaven symbolizes the power to bring about peaceful conditions. The unfolding of the last things is superintended by the God of peace. Even when antagonists show up in the plotline, the story ultimately comes to a peaceful resolution because of "the Lamb" and because of "the throne of God."

Revelation 7 offers a classic portrayal of the gift of a peaceful human life that comes through the reign of God:

> "'Never again will they hunger;
>   never again will they thirst.
> The sun will not beat down on them,'
>   nor any scorching heat.
> For the Lamb at the center of the throne
>   will be their shepherd;
> 'he will lead them to springs of living water.'
>   'And God will wipe away every tear from their eyes.'"
>
> REVELATION 7:16–17

As the story told in Revelation unfolds, the reader is given the sense that someone is in charge, someone who is just and holy, and therefore a peaceful final outcome is assured. The symbolic Babylons of this world, acting in disobedience to God, have no future. That is a peaceful and peacemaking reality. It makes the company of heaven shout:

> "Hallelujah!
> Salvation and glory and power belong to our God,
>   for true and just are his judgments . . .
> Hallelujah!

For our Lord God Almighty reigns.
Let us rejoice and be glad
and give him glory! . . ."

[For he is] KING OF KINGS AND LORD OF LORDS.

REVELATION 19:1–2, 6–7, 16

Though the story includes tension and judgment, we get the sense that something is inevitable:

"The kingdom of the world has become
the kingdom of our Lord and of his Messiah,
and he will reign for ever and ever."

REVELATION 11:15

When Satan is finally and fully defeated, the new heaven and new earth appear. The new Jerusalem and the bride are revealed. Eden is restored. Humanity reigns with God forever. The cosmos finally returns to the peace inherent in our Trinitarian God. We are given this assurance:

The angel said to me, "These words are trustworthy and true. The Lord, the God who inspires the prophets, sent his angel to show his servants the things that must soon take place."
[Jesus adds these words:] "Look, I am coming soon! Blessed is the one who keeps the words of the prophecy written in this scroll."

REVELATION 22:6–7

You will find peace with God and peace within yourself and will be at peace for the world when you know that salvation, moral power, the kingdom of God, and the Messiah are the true, trustworthy, difference-making realities of the world. Not the economy, with its attendant fear; not politics, with its bent to use power to control and corrupt; not entertainment, which can never fully satisfy; and not sex, with its overexaggerated claim on human life. Those things are responsible for creating most of the anxiety in the world. God is peace. His story, with all its ups and downs, ends in perfects peace.

How do you feel as you read these words? Do you hear the invitation to be at peace with God by living into his story through cooperating with the Holy Spirit to become your best "Psalm 139 self"? Would you like to do so?

The Choice to Make Peace with God

The making of choices is a profound aspect of Christian spirituality. In a well-known Old Testament passage, Elijah sought a decision from the people of God: "How long will you waver between two opinions? If the LORD is God, follow him; but if Baal is God, follow him" (1 Kings 18:21).

Similarly, Jesus asked his first friends, "Who do you say I am?" (Matthew 16:15). By asking this question, Jesus alerted his followers to the truth that he was not simply a prophet or a teacher or just another revolutionary. He was the Messiah, the Lord—the one humanity was meant to follow. The chief command of Jesus, the Lord of all, was, "Come, follow me" (Matthew 4:19). The phrase means, "Hither! Behind me!" It was not an invitation to walk side by side as we walk along the way, but rather a command to *come after* or *behind*—as an apprentice to a master. It signified the breaking of ties to all rival demands for loyalty. Its recipients had to decide to follow Jesus as their leader.

The first people to hear this command and to give their lives to following Jesus as Lord started a revolution that continues to this day. They left everything behind. Nothing was too dear to hang on to in the face of the call of Jesus and his kingdom movement. They detached themselves from unneeded consumerism. They set aside self-importance and useless desire. They put the good things of this life (parents, friends, careers, and so forth) in their proper place. They gave up their old life to pick up a superior life as followers of Jesus engaged in kingdom living. In that life, they became even better family members, friends, neighbors, and coworkers.

They found peace with God. They discovered peace within. They were at peace for the world.

At this point in the book, pause and ask yourself, *Do I seek peace with God? Am I ready to follow Jesus?* There can be no compromise here. If you're not ready, that's fine. But take a moment to ask yourself why. Are you waffling about Jesus' worth or his mighty power? Does he not seem worthy of being followed? Does all this "sound good" but not compelling enough yet for you to make a big decision? This is a crucial moment for some intellectual and spiritual honesty. God won't be mad. He knows we live in a spiritually muddy time. He has some experience helping people through puzzling times. Keep it real with God, and see what happens.

In the next two chapters, we'll explore elements of Christlike peace and how we can give ourselves to Jesus as apprentices in peace.

Peace with God: When you think about following Jesus, what aspects of your life seem to battle each other? Can you name specific anxious attitudes or self-incriminating self-talk? How can you set them aside and move more determinedly toward Jesus?

Peace Within: Similar to Lucas and Mia, have you sought peace in unsatisfying ways? Pause to analyze why these methods did not bring the contented peace you had hoped for. What one idea or practice from this chapter do you feel ready to pursue so you can work on finding peace within?

Peace for the Sake of the World: Imagine your life immersed in the peace of the whole story of God—from creation to the amazing scenes we surveyed from the book of Revelation. Can you feel a peaceful confidence? If so, in what specific ways can calm assurance be a springboard to propel you to become a justice creator and a peacemaker?

CHAPTER 7

AN APPRENTICE TO
JESUS IN PEACE

*Peace I leave with you; my peace I give you. I
do not give to you as the world gives. Do not let
your hearts be troubled and do not be afraid.*

JOHN 14.27

At times I look back over my life with significant pessimism.
Over the years I've thought to myself, *I should have been a
baseball coach; I could have helped shape young people.* I have envisioned being a firefighter, thinking I could have served people in
need. I've wondered if I missed the boat by not becoming a professor, imagining I could have assisted students in their careers. When
I'm not having a bad day, and thus not wondering about greener
grass somewhere else, I realize that the truly fundamental aspect of
my life could have been lived out in any role. Because, *fundamentally,* I am a student of Jesus. Apprenticeship to Jesus shapes who I
am. A given role is simply the context in which I learn from Jesus.

Becoming a student of Jesus, the "Prince of Peace" (Isaiah

9:6), is central to possessing and passing on peace. Abiding in peace amid the challenges of life comes through spiritual transformation that is a result of being Jesus' student in kingdom living as he modeled and taught it.

For most of us, this means taking on a new sense of ourselves. It is quite easy to be unconsciously defined by roles, jobs, birth order, or a certain type discovered through personality assessment. We can be defined by the university we attended or by pride in having a blue-collar job that didn't require going to college. We let ourselves be labeled by our neighborhood, our hobbies, our entertainment, or even our pets. These markers of identity, complete with their bumper stickers, T-shirts, or ball caps, can be harmless—just a bit of fun. But for those seeking peace in the way of Jesus, they can never be definitive.

A Passionate Focus

The person seeking peace with God, peace within, and peace for and among others has a passionate focus—to trust and follow Jesus. I want to adopt this focus for myself, because I believe, as N. T. Wright has written, that "God's covenant purpose was to choose a people in and through whom the world would be healed. That purpose, reaching its climax in the Messiah, is now to be worked out through his people."[1]

When we are striving to become people of peace, and when we believe that God is healing the world through us, we naturally arrange the affairs of our lives around that vision. It becomes our clearest, most profound self-identity. This distinctiveness is given shape by habits of the heart that produce confidence in, and apprenticeship to, Jesus. Jesus summarized his invitation this way: "Take my yoke upon you, and learn from me, for I am gentle and humble in heart, and you will find rest for your souls. For my yoke is easy and my burden is light" (Matthew 11:29–30).

The peace that God intends for his people is found in becoming Jesus' student, learning to live a peace-filled, peace-emanating life. God the Father said about Jesus, "This is my Son, whom I love. Listen to him!" (Mark 9:7). We attend to Jesus with the kind of confidence someone has when listening to an art teacher, a golf instructor, a professor, a doctor, or a mechanic. That is to say, we engage Jesus with the deeply held conviction that he knows what he's talking about.

For instance, we come to believe that murder, adultery, divorce, manipulative speech, and revenge seeking (Matthew 5:21–42) are not the things that make for peace. They come from anxiety and conflict. They produce never-ending cycles of angst and war. In contrast, turning the other cheek, settling matters fairly, and going the extra mile (Matthew 5:39–42) are not just fragments of religious rhetoric; they are brilliant insights from the Creator and Sustainer of the universe. They reveal how the world is meant to function.

Jesus comes on the scene and introduces himself by modeling a tightly focused passion: "Do not think that I have come to abolish the Law or the Prophets; I have not come to abolish them but to fulfill them" (Matthew 5:17). When Jesus talks about the Law and the Prophets, he is consciously placing himself in the story that was told of the creation and shaping of Israel, the people of God. The shock is that Jesus interprets that story in himself, saying that his life, his words and works, are announcing, embodying, and demonstrating the full and final work of God on the earth. Jesus is saying, "Look at me; this is the humanity that the Law and the Prophets sought to form." Jesus is humanity, Israel, and the church as God intended.

Jesus and Good Religion

In fulfilling the vision of the Law and the Prophets, Jesus communicated and modeled something much different than the

Pharisees and the teachers of the law focused on. They were trying their best to keep covenant with God. They simply lost their way in their particular way, in their specific era. It's easy for every Christ follower to fail in fidelity to God.

The religious leaders had reduced the universal story of God, shrinking God's intention to religious legalisms and social mores that they categorized, interpreted, ranked, and enforced. It was a recipe for a spiritual and social disaster. And the people knew it. They groaned under the burden of spiritual confusion, economic hardship, social strife, ethnic division, and political approaches that failed to touch true human needs.

In terms of peace, the teaching of the Pharisees and the teachers of the law was a disaster. It created insiders and outsiders, and their way of life fomented disdain for religion and aggravated conflicts among religious and political parties. Their interactions with people were a source of bitter strife and personal anxiety. In their sphere of influence, real peace was alarmingly rare.

In contrast, because of who Jesus was and what he taught, and in response to his loving, wise, and powerful deeds, the people from entire towns often came out to see him. This is the background for scenes like these:

- At the end of the Sermon on the Mount, "the crowds were amazed at his teaching, because he taught as one who had authority, and not as their teachers of the law" (Matthew 7:28–29).
- At the driving out of an impure spirit, "the people were all so amazed that they asked each other, 'What is this? A new teaching—and with authority! He even gives orders to impure spirits and they obey him.' News about him spread quickly over the whole region of Galilee" (Mark 1:27–28).
- The temple guards, stunned by the clarity and power of

Jesus' teaching, said, "No one ever spoke the way this man does" (John 7:46).

- When Jesus was teaching at a festival, "the Jews there were amazed and asked, 'How did this man get such learning without having been taught?' Jesus answered, 'My teaching is not my own. It comes from the one who sent me'" (John 7:15–16).

Jesus' teaching provides a welcome and stark contrast to his contemporaries. He explained reality, which was freeing to people. They could feel the spiritual release in comparison to the bondage of civil religion. Peace is found in such freedom. Peaceful people pass it on. They become peacemakers. Jesus called them "blessed" and said such people are examples of those who are the "children of God" (Matthew 5:9). Religion cannot reliably produce peace in a human heart, but the life of Jesus in a heart will surely do so.

This is why we apprentice ourselves to Jesus in pursuit of peace. He not only knows about peace—like teachers know their subjects—but actually experienced peace within conflict and tribulation. He never fought back on the terms of this world. Jesus thus modeled peaceableness to others and invited us to become his students, learning to live our lives in peace in the manner in which he did.

Life's Purpose: Being a Disciple of Jesus

Finlay had lost his way. As he was preparing for university, his dad encouraged him to pursue a field of study that would guarantee a good job upon graduation. Finlay did just that, selecting construction engineering. He came to enjoy his courses. Far from seeing just the economic benefits, he was enthusiastic about making a contribution to the physical world that was both useful and beautiful. But Finlay had the grave misfortune of graduating during the recession of 2008. No one was building or renovating anything. No one would even look at his résumé, saying: "Come back later, when the economy recovers."

Finlay wasn't bitter at the way his dad's advice was turning out. Nor did he regret his degree choice. The problem was that the path of life had suddenly disappeared in front of him. The trail was no longer marked. Frozen with indecision, he lost purpose. "Who am I now?" was his nightly troubled question.

Knowing who we are and knowing what our life's purpose is are crucial aspects of peace with God, peace within, and peace for the sake of the world. Christians are meant, no matter what other roles we play, to apprentice ourselves to Jesus and become instruments of peace.

Seeking Cruciformity

Peace and self-will do not mix. Willfulness wins, and peace loses. This is true because continually insisting on one's way requires force—a force that often comes in the shape of bullying, manipulating, and deceiving others. We cannot imagine that peace could survive in that kind of environment. But the answer is not to swing wildly in the opposite direction. Peace does not mean becoming a doormat for everyone to walk on. It doesn't mean the loss of desire or the suppression of our own perspective on a given matter. It doesn't mean inactivity in the face of injustice. There is an in-between place, a bull's-eye. The target for spiritual health is that our God-given will is reshaped. N. T. Wright gives a vision for cross-shaped transformation:

> The cross is the surest, truest and deepest window on the
> very heart and character of the living and loving God; the
> more we learn about the cross . . . the more we discover about
> the One in whose image we are made and hence about our

own vocation to be the cross-bearing people, the people in whose lives and service the living God is made known.[2]

The practices leading to cruciform living are not natural; they must be learned. What are the conventional wisdoms out of which we operate that bring conflict rather than peace? Let's explore some common issues that work against cruciformity.

Winning at all costs. This is an attitude, a posture of the heart and a bent of the will, that believes no matter how much damage or pain I cause to a person or entity, my behavior is justified by the importance of winning. What if you are the recipient of this no-holds-barred practice? How scary is it to be treated as if nothing is off the table? How would you feel, knowing someone has no qualms about treating you in that manner? This attitude believes that when something is important enough, when we are absolutely certain about being in the right, all restraints of decency can be cast off. Right and wrong no longer need to be considered—winning is what is right. Winning at all costs means we don't have to pay attention to rules; rules are for the weak, after all. But those who don't care about rules will do whatever it takes to win, like cheating and lying.

Winning at all costs is tragically shortsighted. It is a common way to lose at life. It causes long-term collateral damage to family, friends, coworkers, and reputation. Listening, as an act of caring, goes out the window. Collaboration and community are made impossible. Trust is ruined. Integrity, honor, and character are shattered. Everyone in our orb is put on the defensive. We become our own worst enemy as our instincts and behaviors kill our relationships and careers. Our selfishness chases away peace, and violence, abuse, and intimidation take its place.

We may be tempted to think, *Surely no Christian would ever act in this manner!* I wish I could agree. But sadly, often it is precisely religious or spiritual aims—motives of supreme importance—that are often used to justify winning at all costs. I've seen it in families, among peers, and in church council meetings, and we see it in the reports of brutal acts of ideologically fueled violence that regularly appear in our newsfeeds.

Responding to others with contempt. To hold someone in contempt is to think of them as unworthy of respect and maybe even undeserving of our attention. It is to scorn others or to think of them as beneath us, if not totally worthless. Followers of Jesus cultivate positive love for others. Followers of Jesus who are pursuing peace don't visualize getting back at people. They don't daydream about how to "put people in their place," harm them through retribution, or ruin their reputation. They don't fantasize about how to bring them down a peg or two. Rather, disciples of Jesus wonder about these things:

- What is the source of this contempt?
- Why do I allow contempt to reside in my heart?
- Does contempt fit well with peace, with loving my neighbor or my enemy?
- Do I enjoy the feeling of contempt—is it pleasurable to me?
- Does contempt give me a sense of having a superior place or greater power?

Contempt can be upon us before we can stop it. Feelings are involuntary and spontaneous. Though they're not directly under our control, we don't need to be controlled by them.

When we feel sucked in by feelings, we can simply step out of the suction—like unplugging the vacuum cleaner when something gets stuck in the rolling brushes. Followers of Jesus come to learn that our feelings do not have to be fulfilled. We aren't ruled by them; we are ruled by God and his kingdom. We don't have to spend time griping about not getting what we want; rather, we pray, "Lord, your kingdom come, your will be done." We joyfully, in peace, let God be God and invite him to superintend our lives and the affairs of the whole world.

At its core, the quest for peace involves apprenticing one's self to Jesus. As disciples of Jesus, we learn to recognize our personal sources of anxiety and conflict. Denial or suppression of who we are and what we spontaneously feel cannot lead to healing, to peace within. We seek to replace disordered desires with the fundamental elements of faith—loving God and loving (working for the good) of our neighbors and our enemies. We don't want our feelings to become the sole reason or main justification for our actions. That simply imprisons us in our feelings. Through spiritual transformation into Christlikeness, we aim at the Spirit-inspired fruit of self-control. We seek the ability to do what is good and just, even if such actions run contrary to our temporary, instinctive feelings. For most of us, this ability requires a substantial makeover of our heart, soul, mind, and emotions.

Entering God's kingdom and discovering a regenerated life is possible. Countless human beings have done so. Jesus invites us, and the Spirit stands ready to enable us, to seek and experience a life healed and made free in the kingdom of God. In response, we take the small, humble, grace-based, and Spirit-enabled steps that gently and surely lead to the ability to live in peace in a given moment. Our goal as apprentices of Jesus in lives of peace is not merely to avoid acts of sin but to become the kind of persons who, because of a profound, controlling desire to love God and others, are not tempted to or disposed to adopt peace-killing attitudes and actions. As students of Jesus, we have turned our desires away from the things that produce conflict to the things that make for peace—ours and others'.

We need a shift in perspective: in the plan of God, each one of us exists for others, who now become the objects of our selfless love. That truth changes everything—if we want it to. If we are willing to engage in the renovation of our hearts. If we are willing to give ourselves over to a lifestyle of repentance, of aligning our hearts to the heart of Jesus. In return, a profoundly wonderful future awaits us, as Dallas Willard taught: "Love, joy, and peace fostered in divine fellowship simply crowd out fear, anger, unsatisfied desire, woundedness, rejection. There is no longer room for them."[3] Thus, cultivating love, joy, and peace is the indirect strategy for overcoming feelings that lead us away from God and toward harming ourselves or mistreating others.

Serving as an Instrument of Peace

Those who have become followers of Jesus are simultaneously chosen to be instruments of God and thus *instruments of peace*. We get a glimpse of this in Jesus' interaction with the woman in the crowd who touched his clothes because she believed she would be healed by doing so (Mark 5:25–28). She had suffered some kind of menstrual blood loss for twelve years, and it had made her an outcast in society. She had little ability to act on her own behalf and had suffered greatly as she sought a cure. Jesus told her, "Daughter, your faith has healed you. Go in peace and be freed from your suffering" (Mark 5:34).

What do you think Jesus had in mind when he pictured the now healed woman going in peace, finally *being at peace*? Two sources of terrible harassment are almost sure to have clung to this woman over the twelve years of her torment: anxiety and conflict.

Imagine having a chronic headache that remained undiagnosed and therefore was incapable of being treated. Anxious fears of brain cancer or some other terrible disease would surely pop up. What's more, the woman healed by Jesus also would have been anxious about the social barrier erected between her and her friends due to her unrelenting blood loss. It even would have put a strain on her family: How could they care for her without becoming unclean themselves? She would have been worried about putting her family in a no-win situation.

In terms of conflict, what do you think it would have been like to deal with the quacks who promised healing but only took her money and dignity? She likely was rejected, abused, and shunned. She couldn't approach anyone and ask to be in a relationship. To do so would have been out-of-bounds socially, as well as sinful in religious terms.

She was stuck, conflicted within and without. I love the thought that in the gracious purposes of Jesus her healed body also gave her a quiet mind. While I'm sure she was thankful beyond words to notice that her bleeding had stopped, I'll bet in the hours and days that followed she was equally grateful that the roiling mayhem of her mind had ceased.

Made well and infused with peace, this woman now needed to take her place in the world as a source of peace.

Growing in Qualities of Peace

What should we think of as the portrait of a person at peace? What qualities of being are we shooting for? Here are a few brief ideas to get us started.

Peace-loving. Differentiating between divine wisdom and what we might call the wisdom of the street, James wrote, "But the wisdom that comes from heaven is first of all pure; then *peace-loving*, considerate, submissive, full of mercy and good fruit, impartial and sincere" (James 3:17, emphasis mine). James is alerting us to the notion that loving peace, seeking peace, and positioning oneself to receive and live in peace are a part of divine wisdom, part of God's intention for humanity. We were built to seek, find, and embody peace in our way of life. While this desire may seem buried in sin, it is nonetheless in our DNA to do so. We can find peace via the route marked by Psalm 34:14: "Turn from evil and do good; seek peace and pursue it."

Put on the yoke of Jesus and learn from him what the long story of the Bible is all about—God's creation of people who are conspicuous for their love, joy, hope, and peace—all for the sake of serving others. As you do, you will see that Jesus really knows what he's talking about; he is pointing to something fundamental about peace when he says, "Come to me . . . Take my yoke upon you and learn from me, for I am gentle and humble in heart," and as you do, "you will find rest" (Matthew 11:28–29).

A significant part of such rest comes from having a heart at peace instead of a disordered heart that constantly screams for attention, requiring us to manage it closely. Ask any manager: managing is tough and exhausting work. Having to manage an angry, lustful, covetous, mean, and judgmental heart will wear us out, leaving us with no energy to love or serve others. In contrast, a heart at peace in the midst of troublesome events exploding all around it experiences a potent stillness that can be shared with others. As the psalmist writes, "Great peace have those who love your law, and nothing can make them stumble" (Psalm 119:165).

Standing firm through the experience of great peace allows us to do the good we dream about doing—to catch, uphold, and mend those who stumble and fall.

Peaceable. Paul told Titus that a part of his pastoral work was "to be *peaceable* and considerate, and always to be gentle toward everyone" (Titus 3:1–2, emphasis mine). Paul had in mind the way the overflow of our lives in Christ can be applied to the good of others, for the benefit of society. What Jesus was in his place and time—an agent of rescue and healing—we are to be in our place and time.

Peaceful. As Paul mentored Timothy in life and ministry, he told Timothy to pray "that we may live *peaceful* and quiet lives in all godliness and holiness" (1 Timothy 2:2, emphasis mine). *Peaceful* envisions a life that is undisturbed and does not disturb others; that is quiet, not obnoxious; pleasant, not disagreeable;

calm, not agitating. *Peaceful* calls to mind the kind of person whose first impulse is to welcome, build bridges, think about what is best for others, not to reject or to engage in conflict.

Peacemaking. Jesus said, "Blessed are the *peacemakers*, for they will be called children of God" (Matthew 5:9, emphasis mine). Eugene Peterson's rendering in *The Message* is particularly helpful: "You're blessed when you can show people how to cooperate instead of compete or fight." James adds to Jesus' thoughts a vision of the outcome of peacemaking: "*Peacemakers* who sow in peace reap a harvest of righteousness" (James 3:18, emphasis mine). Peacemakers bring peace.

But this peace is not always peace*keeping*, if by this we mean keeping things as they are. We'll explore this nuance in more depth in coming chapters, but for now let's just consider that peace*making* is a verb—a livable action. Peacemakers (Greek, *eirenopoios*, from the root *eiro*, which means "to join") bind up or join together to make whole again that which is broken, divided, or separated. Peacemakers seek reconciliation, and as they do, they avoid words or actions that are harmful or divisive. In this way, we are called "children of God" and "reap a harvest of righteousness." Through this kind of life, we both are *at peace*—not fighting inwardly or outwardly—and *make peace* in the situations of our lives, exhibiting life-giving graciousness and generosity.

Peace-loving . . . peaceable . . . peaceful . . . peacemaking—these are attractive qualities worthy of our pursuit. But such a quest is easier said than done. There are battles inside and conflicts outside. Every day, the news and our social media outlets give us things to mourn or to worry about or to be angry about. There are many reasons to feel anxious or to engage in constant conflict with those with whom we disagree. The world is always telling one story, but those who seek peace live in an alternative story.

And so the church is presented with a challenge: to embrace a way of being a Christ follower that looks like a cross-shaped loss, not like a victory. N. T. Wright says that the story of Israel "was never about Israel beating up her enemies and becoming established as the high-and-mighty masters of the world."[4] Wright's insight about Israel confronts the church as well: *"[Jesus'] kingdom-agenda for Israel demanded that Israel leave off her frantic and paranoid self-defense . . . and embrace instead the vocation to be the light of the world, the salt of the earth."*[5]

Apprenticing ourselves to Jesus is our peace. And following Jesus is always for the sake of others. In the next chapter, we'll seek alignment to the Jesus of justice.

Peace with God: Sometimes peace with God escapes us because we are fighting against a cross-shaped life. Are you fighting with God along these lines? If so, identify the reasons as clearly as you can. Confess to God what you discover. Stick with it until you begin to feel both pardon for sin and hope for freedom.

Peace Within: What do you most admire about the peaceful way Jesus conducted his life? Imagine yourself living that way. What practices can you take on to head in that direction? Ask the Spirit to help you discover your next steps.

Peace for the Sake of the World: Can you identify times in your life when self-focus makes serving others difficult? See if you can recognize the underlying drivers: Fear? Feelings of awkwardness? A desire to avoid risk? Make a decision to ignore default positions. Make a plan to adopt new attitudes and actions in your real world. Notice how you feel during these occasions, and adjust as you grow in understanding.

CHAPTER 8

THE JESUS OF JUSTICE, MERCY, AND HUMILITY

Peace can never be built on the foundation of Greed and Oppression.

JULIA MAY COURTNEY, "REMEMBER
LUDLOW!" *MOTHER EARTH*

The road to holiness necessarily passes through the world of action.

DAG HAMMARSKJÖLD, *MARKINGS*

The only order and peace that God desires is that which is based on truth and justice.

ARCHBISHOP OSCAR ROMERO,
"HOMILY: CHRIST, LIFE AND
TREASURE FOR ALL," JULY 1, 1979

When the disruptive power of COVID-19 became clear in early 2020, my strong instinct was to care for the clergy, since as bishop in the Anglican Church I have the responsibility to oversee. I was especially concerned about the rapidly increasing division caused by the partisan political rhetoric of the 2020 election cycle. Daily I witnessed harsh, dehumanizing hostility happening in families, friendships, workplaces, schools, churches, and neighborhoods.

On a societal level, the people I consulted with in senior national law enforcement and veteran thinkers in Washington politics were significantly concerned about the possibility of armed conflict among radicals in the streets of America. I thought to myself, *Dueling AR-15 rifles help no one. Healing the hearts of potential shooters helps every human being.* My focus on the hearts of people felt justified and aligned with Jesus' teaching that what we say and do come out of the overflow of our hearts (Luke 6:45).

Thus, much of my writing and social media posts during the first months of 2020 focused on internal, attitudinal issues. I was sincerely trying to cultivate respect, patience, generosity of spirit, and ways to stay in the room with difference. But in the middle of what I had been observing and naming, the crucial issue of race came up. Though I care about racial issues, I did not give them equal emphasis. They did not show up on my social media platforms. I regret this. My actions are a classic case of overemphasizing internal issues of peace. While I was seeking relational calm, which is good for people of any ethnicity, others were seeking deliverance from cultural suffocation. The icon of this was the knee of a White police officer on the neck of a Black man.[1]

I don't think I was entirely wrong to give my audience an imagination for becoming truly good, kind, and generous people. After all, this is part of what the Bible means when it refers to *righteousness*. But with the benefit of hindsight, I'm now also learning to take in the whole meaning of righteousness, which includes bringing justice to bear for those oppressed in various ways. I found myself needing to take a fresh look at the Jesus of justice, to embody the words of William Penn: "True godliness does not turn [people] out of the world, but enables them to live better in it and excites their endeavors to mend it."[2]

Richard Foster, speaking of the intersection of Spirit power and social engagement, helps us realize a central truth: "The [Spirit] power to be the kind of people we were created to be and the power to do the works of God upon the earth places us on solid ground to engage the demands of the social arena. And no place is in greater need of people full of the Holy Spirit and divine love."[3]

In *Evil and the Justice of God*, N. T. Wright examines how Abraham and the people of God, as God's agents of justice, did not always get it right. Chapter 2 contains a section called "People of the Solution, People of the Problem."[4] When I first saw it, I wrote in the margin of my book, "That's me too!" I'd like to get to the place where I can pray with the fervor of Dorothy Day: "There I offered up a special prayer—a prayer which came with tears and with anguish, that some way would open for me to use what talents I possessed for my fellow workers, for the poor."[5]

When issues of race, immigration, or economic justice are in view, many of us need a Jesus-based freedom from fear of engagement. The nervous confusion from politically loaded terminology is not at all helpful. It obscures more than it reveals. It's like using a sledgehammer to put a tack in a bulletin board.

The events of 2020—and a few loyal colleagues—have taught me that no matter what biblical and theological issues one is working though, *seeking peace* calls for us to get to a place where we consistently give issues of injustice the prioritized focus they deserve. This is what it means to be peacemakers in the world. And we are called to be Jesus people who are embedded in our

actual time, with all of its real and specific issues (race, immigration, sexuality, economics, and so forth).

Ignoring justice is not an option for followers of Jesus who
seek to live in and extend peace. Evil must be named and properly
opposed. To do so does not come naturally to me. My number one
strength on the CliftonStrengths assessment tool is "positivity."[6]
I don't like negative things, and negative people aren't the easiest
folks for me to interact with. I'm still working it out, but I wonder
if issues of justice have just been too negative for me—maybe my
need to see everything positively just can't handle them.

In addition, the evangelicalism in which I came to faith and
developed early forms of maturity did not value issues of justice.
We valued helping people find forgiveness so they would go to
heaven when they died. It was the dreaded *liberals* who focused
on justice. For them, the whole gospel was about social justice.
They came to this conclusion while simultaneously throwing out
much of orthodox Christian revelation. That caricature is a bit
oversimplified, but it was the understanding of my youth.

These days I would say that going to heaven is not the gospel.
Nor is simply doing justice. The gospel according to Jesus is that
God's reign is with us (Mark 1:14–15). His reign in our lives calls
for repentance and belief. Discipleship is interactive apprenticeship to Jesus through the Holy Spirit. Discipleship, so construed,
is the core calling of the gospel. It will indeed lead us to peace
in this life and to heaven in the life to come. But it also calls us
to "act justly and to love mercy and to walk humbly with [our]
God" (Micah 6:8).

Oscar Romero helps me imagine this: "When we preach the
Lord's word, we decry not only the injustices of the social order.
We decry every sin that is night, that is darkness: drunkenness,
gluttony, lust, adultery, abortion, everything that is the reign of
iniquity and sin."[7] Romero was looking to wake people up to
whole-life conversion. His teachings remind us not to be wicked

and cruel; not to do injustice, hate others, or seek revenge; to love and serve others and pursue their freedom. He knew that *church* is a holistic term that includes spiritual formation and justice. He taught that "without love justice is only the sword."[8]

Romero was aware that there is a difference between the liberation brought by the church and "liberations that are only political and temporal."[9] He wrote, "Let us not just shout slogans about new structures; new structures will be worthless without new persons to administer the new structures."[10] Romero challenges me with the notion that we have to live in our moment of history, with all its complexities, and that "those preachers who avoid every thorny matter so as not to be harassed, so as not to have conflicts and difficulties, do not light up the world they live in."[11]

The Kingdom of God Is Justice and Peace

The lyrics of the lovely Taizé chorus I quoted to begin this chapter expose an important truth: peace sits alongside justice as a priority of God. The kingdom of God is justice *and* peace. The church often breaks this creative tension. The tendency of much of Christian spirituality is to focus on personal piety over issues of justice. In a few cases, the script is flipped, and Jesus is seen as only a social revolutionary who doesn't care much about the human heart, spirituality, or eternity.

Of course, for Jesus, issues of the heart are crucial (Luke 6:45). As we follow Jesus as his student-disciples, we indeed take on a renewed heart. But one's heart never exists in isolation. A Jesus-like heart is a social reality meant to overflow in Jesus-like deeds—caring for the least, the last, the left out. This is why Jesus so often criticized the religious rulers of his day, who focused on law keeping, while Jesus focused on healing for the various ways people are oppressed and exploited.

Some Issues of Spiritual Formation Can Only Be Learned While Pursuing Justice

Formation and justice work together. In terms of spiritual growth, the poor teach the nonpoor. Elizabeth O'Connor wrote, "They don't let you be phony with them. They live closer to reality—to death and life and despair and hope. The poor have less to hide behind. There is no cushion of money and things to help them appear to themselves and to others what they are not"[12] The message here is that *some elements of spiritual formation can only be learned in the pursuit of justice*—and also that works of justice are demonstrated best by a transformed heart.

We can only be whole and at peace when we take seriously the dynamic tension between social justice deeds and contemplation/formation. Some of us who are action oriented just want to get on with the work. But often we do so without using careful discernment and establishing good practices for self-care and team building. Others seek the mystical benefits of retreat, of silence and solitude, of *being*, not *doing*.

This conflict resides both in our hearts and in our faith communities. We don't break the tension in one way or the other. Like two notes played simultaneously and in tune, we harmonize justice and formation. We strive for this coherence because "the outward journey and the inward journey are inextricably bound together."[13]

Show and Tell

Think about all that the disciples saw Jesus do—healing people, delivering them, raising the dead, calming the wind and waves, releasing the oppressed—and all that they heard him teach and all that they witnessed regarding the way he peacefully yet influentially and compellingly carried himself in the world as an agent of healing. For our work here, we may hear Jesus say, "Keep doing what you saw and heard from me. Keep the Jesus movement going. As you do, you can count on the Holy Spirit to lead you along the way."

We will think more about the Spirit in the chapters to come, but for now we need to hold tight to the notion that the person and work of the Holy Spirit are central and normative to Christian spirituality. He is not optional. He is not just for those who "seek something more." God's work within you, birthing peace and bringing justice, comes only through an interactive relationship with the Holy Spirit. The Jesus movement—which came into being through the work of the Spirit in Mary (Matthew 1:18)—has now grown into the Jesus-Spirit movement.

God gave Mary a vision and an understanding for what the Spirit was birthing in her—the Magnificat. As we might guess, Mary, anticipating the work of God in Jesus Christ, clearly sees a mix of justice and peace:

> His mercy extends to those who fear him,
>   from generation to generation.
> He has performed mighty deeds with his arm;
>   he has scattered those who are proud in their inmost
>   thoughts.
> He has brought down rulers from their thrones
>   but has lifted up the humble.
> He has filled the hungry with good things
>   but has sent the rich away empty.
>
> LUKE 1:50–53

The justice and peace work of Jesus revealed by Mary is carried on by Christians. For instance, when the apostles were questioned by the authorities about healing those who were lame (Acts 4:5–12), Peter, filled with the Holy Spirit (v. 8), said that their act of kindness arose in and through the Jesus/Spirit movement (v. 10). The Spirit chose deacons who served the world (Acts 6:5). The Spirit-enabled Jesus movement was kept aflame by the Spirit: "Then the church throughout Judea, Galilee and Samaria enjoyed a time of peace and was strengthened. Living in the fear of the Lord and encouraged by the Holy Spirit, it increased in numbers" (Acts 9:31).

The Jesus movement, with all its far-reaching effects on social justice and its creation of personal and relational peace, begins with and is carried along by the person and work of the Holy Spirit. John the Baptist said, "After me comes one who is more powerful than I, whose sandals I am not worthy to carry. He will baptize you with the Holy Spirit and fire" (Matthew 3:11).

Formed in Peace for the Good

We began this chapter with my confession of a recent deepening of my understanding of how calling for peace and working for justice go together. In that time period, I found myself wondering, *How might we be formed for* the good? Not surprisingly, such attentiveness took me to the classic, paradigm-shaping words found in Micah 6:8 (NRSV):

> He has told you, O mortal, what is good;
>   and what does the LORD require of you
>   but to do justice, and to love kindness,
>   and to walk humbly with your God?

Micah appears to have a few things motivating him: a strong ache for societal justice, a critique of a pietistic religion expressed in mere offerings, and a prophetic call for Israel to keep the demands of her covenant with Yahweh. Micah was dealing with a people "who would offer everything, . . . excepting what alone

God asked for, their heart, its love and its obedience . . . Israel ritualistically recited their creeds, but because they refused to live by a faith that risks itself in doing justice, they never comprehended their meaning."[14] Micah was insisting that a person who does not practice mercy and justice in covenant solidarity with fellow human beings has never participated in the covenant of grace.[15]

Micah's well-known thoughts give me a vision that God's people can walk, chew gum, and naturally swing their arms all at the same time. An individual life *can*—and is indeed *required to*—engage in a three-part simultaneity: do justice, love mercy, walk humbly. We don't have to settle for something *mere*, such as mere justice without humility, or mere humility (formation) without kindness and just actions.

If we sit with the text for a bit, a few lovely thoughts emerge that give us a vision for one whole life *formed in peace* for *justice.*

First, the text stands up to be noticed and calls out, "Hey, humanity, *you have been told.*" What Yahweh wants should be prominently visible and regularly practiced in the life of the community. Micah was not repudiating sacrifice or what we today call worship. He subordinated it to ethics. He pressed for "a spiritual commitment to God and one another as evidenced by doing justice."[16]

A comprehensive definition of "what is good" comes next. It is a good that is moral because it aligns with the will of God in creation. And this good is knowable and livable. The text names three actions that manifest *the good* that God intends to be achieved through his elect, covenanted, Spirit-filled people.

1. Do justice. To do justice is to sort out what belongs to whom and to give it back, thus delivering the oppressed from their oppression.[17] It means to return the things that have been stolen from the oppressed: life, freedom, agency, and power. Justice calls for restoring identity, peace and quiet, dignity, security, and the

like. It is a reordering of reality such that the victims of injustice are made whole again in a dynamic, transformative manner.

To act in these ways, we must seek the reformation of our hearts away from fear, consumerism, insecurity, and instinctually unfair, angry judgments. Many of us will be summoned to show courage, to acknowledge that which has been purposely or inadvertently repressed.

2. Love kindness (Hebrew, *hesed*; mercy; Yahweh's covenant love). The authors of *To Act Justly, Love Tenderly, Walk Humbly* write, "Yahweh's covenant love was tender, but tenacious; fierce and intensely determined."[18] This is the posture we are given for our social engagement. Coming to love the covenant love of God is what produces mercy and loving-kindness in us, which then spills over into acts of agape and justice.

While feelings of empathy and compassion are obviously commendable, the command here is not simply to *feel* something akin to *hesed*. Rather, the command to "love *hesed*" is an appeal to move from indifference to the engaging of our will, desires, and spiritual motivations so that they animate mercy and justice. It implies providing or protecting space in which the good can occur. It connotes a tight connection between the affections of the heart (the inner person) and one's bodily action in the world. *Love* is a "doing" word that points toward a respectful, faithful, and generous keeping of covenant with God. Loving mercy and doing mercy are the natural fruit of cherishing God's work on earth and treasuring the oppressed.

The vision of Isaiah summarizes agape-based justice and mercy as "to loose the bonds of injustice, to undo the thongs of the yoke, to let the oppressed go free, and to break every yoke" (Isaiah 58:6 NRSV).

Loving mercy has the characteristic of *solidarity* associated with it, along with the notion of neighborliness (see Luke 10, the parable of the good Samaritan). The solidarity envisioned is patient, attentive, waiting, hoping.[19] But it also pursues love-based active intervention that creates real, meaningful change toward justice. This can be challenging when our congregations are divided about issues of race and we're trying to set a good pace of change for those just entering the race conversation. To discern the way forward, we need to keep the whole of humanity in view: one person's (slow) pace is an agony for the one oppressed. The one who is drowning is *in a hurry* to be rescued.

3. **Walk humbly.** *Walking* points to our whole manner of being in the world—the way we carry ourselves and our mode or style of living. Learning to walk with God in humility and meekness is core to both the process and goal of spiritual trans-formation into Christlikeness. It is the bent of the heart that underlies practices of mercy and justice.

Doing justice and mercy in humility means we move from acts of leadership or service that are "power over" to a self-emptying "presence with."[20] It means we are intentionally conscious of the fact that those we seek to deliver from injustice are never objects but are subjects with dignity, agency, wills, and purposes of their own.

Walking humbly (wisely and thoughtfully) with the Author of the covenant is the source of one's ability to love kindness and to do justice. This is where formation in Christlikeness, Jesus' kingdom message, and the practice of doing justice come together in sweet harmony in one holistic life. I seek such a life. All places and eras have their own versions of "orphans and widows" (James 1:27)—the broken, despised, helpless, and undefended.[21] Caring for them is true religion.

Doing Justice to Justice

Isaiah 61:8 gives a clear basis for working for justice: "For I, the LORD, love justice." Justice is a *biblical* issue. We cannot let it be owned or shaped or have its outcomes defined by partisan politics. Neither should any ongoing political quarreling shut us down. Given that these scenarios are happening all around us, what manner of being, what sort of person, best does justice to justice? Approaches to justice can themselves be unjust—brute force, coercion, manipulation, abuse of power, and the like. On the contrary, the great Christian masters on the topic of justice agree that godly ends must employ godly means. On Micah's terms, this means that in order to do justice to justice, we need to simultaneously love kindness and walk humbly.

Micah's three-pronged approach reveals that social justice cannot be done without caring for the condition of one's heart at the same time. In my long career, I have observed many instances of justice workers who became burned-out by not accepting limitations but instead trying to do too much, by becoming rigid and being rude to those who didn't see what they saw or didn't live up to their standards, by acting unkindly or working in fear-based ways, by becoming overly enmeshed in partisan politics, or by being judgmental. The wise teacher Richard Foster wrote, "Service that is duty-motivated breathes death. Service that flows out of our inward person is life, and joy and peace."[22]

On Jesus' terms, the basis of justice is to love our neighbors and our enemies and to practice the Golden Rule. In the Pauline vision of ethics for the people of God, we are to seek justice in ways that "let [our] gentleness [considerateness, reasonableness, moderation] be evident to all" (Philippians 4:5). We do justice best as we invite the Spirit to work his fruit in us: "love, joy, peace, forbearance, kindness, goodness, faithfulness, gentleness and self-control" (Galatians 5:22–23). Paul's vision was that the church would carry out its call to do justice "with all humility and gentleness, with patience, bearing with one another in love, eager to maintain the unity of the Spirit in the bond of peace" (Ephesians 4:2–3 ESV).

Those Spirit-inspired qualities of our being make for the inner movement within our souls that results in deeds of kindness, generosity, and justice. We want servant hearts, not just servant actions. We want to replace the legalistic *I ought to* or *I should* with the overflow of a heart animated by *I want to* and *I get to* use my creative gifts for the sake of liberating others.

The lesson that is deepening in me is this: spiritual formation is honed in the midst of mission. As Richard Foster phrased it, "Nothing *disciplines* the inordinate desires of the flesh like service, and nothing *transforms* the desires of the flesh like serving in hiddenness. The flesh whines against service but screams against hidden service."[23]

A proper heart ethic *within* must be accompanied by action *without*. Working from peaceful souls, disciples of Jesus live with an others-oriented love in our hearts and a towel in our hands (John 13:1–17). As James put it, "Faith without deeds is dead" (James 2:26). Paul insists that we are "created in Christ Jesus for good works, which God prepared beforehand to be our way of life" (Ephesians 2:10 NRSV). This is the vision of practical obedience to Jesus that takes us outward beyond our fears, our doubts regarding our ability to make a difference, our self-focus, our own needs.

Any bold adventure toward mission or in the direction of justice will naturally involve risk-taking. Taking risks for justice, because it intends to shatter the status quo and shake up stereotypes, always carries with it the unknown. The unknown produces no small amount of anxiety and self-doubt. But as Elizabeth O'Connor wrote, "When we do not allow ourselves the possibility of failure, the Spirit cannot work in us."[24] It is the person and work of the Holy Spirit in power, fruit, and gifts that give us the capacity to carry on, to keep working at a big vision like cooperating with the Jesus/Spirit movement in bringing about justice and peace. Gordon Cosby, founder of Church of the Savior in Washington, D.C., said, "The Scriptures on gifts that we find in Romans, Corinthians, and Ephesians contain spiritual dynamite. If we will take them seriously, they will set off a revolution in the churches that will bring in a whole new age of the Spirit."[25]

If we choose to follow Jesus in the way of justice and peace, the Spirit of peace will need to work powerfully within us. We'll explore the Spirit of peace in the next chapter.

Peace with God: In this chapter, we noted that Isaiah 61:8 declares that the Lord "loves justice." To have peace with God, our loves and our desires must harmonize with his love for justice. Can you name one or two current desires of your heart that are not in harmony with God's love of justice?

Peace Within: In this chapter, I shared a glimpse of my journey in drawing a closer link between internal matters of peace and societal problems of justice. Can you relate to my growth? How so? What is your story? Can you recount it to God and ask him to change your heart and your mind wherever it may be needed?

Peace for the Sake of the World: What is your dream for justice and peace? What is it saying to you? How is it moving you? Whom do you need to tell? Is something holding you back? What is the first step?

CHAPTER 9

THE SPIRIT OF PEACE

The mind governed by the Spirit is life and peace.

ROMANS 8:6

Holy Spirit, teach me to be your gentle follower in all situations.

N. T. WRIGHT

When I was president of a large nonprofit, we had to raise a lot of money. I felt the pressure. I ached under the grind. Along the way, two donors, both with high capacity and good intelligence, saw what was going on and offered help. "Todd," they said, "do your best, and we'll make up the rest. We love the work you're doing, and we will be your backstop." *Backstop*— what a freeing idea! Suddenly I felt safe. It was also inspiring. It made me and the team all the more diligent in our fundraising. Someone had our back.

God backs *your* act. His backing is a vital source of inner and relational peace. It means you don't need to have your own back. The Spirit, as various texts translate the Greek term *parakletos*, is the *Comforter*, the *Helper*, the *Comforting Counselor*, the *Companion*, the *Advocate*. Imagine those names representing God's activity in your life—comforting, helping, counseling, companioning, and advocating. Receiving the Spirit means we can ditch the anxious energy we use to motivate our work or to protect ourselves. We can put that formerly wasted energy to peaceful use as we love and serve others.

It is through the person and work of the Holy Spirit that God upholds our life. Thus, an ongoing, honest, and robust conversational relationship with the Spirit is crucial to Christian spirituality. A faith-filled, welcoming interaction with the Spirit is the basis a life of peace and justice. The Holy Spirit is not optional—like a tech, safety, or touring package on a new car.

The Holy Spirit is not owned or defined by a denomination or era of church history. The Spirit cannot be reduced to a religious consumer choice: "I'm really Presbyterian, Baptist, Methodist, Lutheran, or Anglican, but I guess I'll have *a bit* of the Spirit"—as if the Spirit is a side dish to the main course of denominational affiliation. The Holy Spirit is Almighty God, the third person of the Holy Trinity. The Holy Spirit deserves our love, respect, and obedience, not suspicion and cynicism. Having confidence in the work of the Spirit and taking him seriously is vital to peace in life and ministry. Seeking the Spirit is what finds the Spirit, not just being *open*, as if God has something to prove to you—and you might be willing to give him a break if he acts the way you require him to.

Whether or not we perceive it, we live, by God's design and purpose, in the age of the Holy Spirit. Discipleship to Jesus and our church life are meant to have at their center an interactive relationship with the Holy Spirit. Why? I put it this way: "God's purposes in full-orbed, others-oriented, missional discipleship require a power that matches his intentions. This power comes from the person and work of the Holy Spirit."[1]

This is why Jesus said to his first followers, "I am going to send you what my Father has promised; but stay in the city until you have been *clothed with power* from on high" (Luke 24:49, emphasis mine). This definitive idea is meant to be a reality for Christian life. The power of the Spirit is central to all the good we feel called to do in the world.

The Holy Spirit moves us to be and do in the manner of Jesus. Think of the quality of life that Jesus knew, his inward experience of love, joy, and peace—this is the work the Spirit does in us.

The Holy Spirit presents Jesus to us in our minds and hearts and continues the personal presence and ministry of Jesus within the church. The Holy Spirit gives the church its sense of authorization to work on God's behalf in the world. Jesus closely connected peace, the *sentness* of the church, and the power of the Holy Spirit. Among his last words to the disciples were these: "'Peace be with you! As the Father has sent me, I am sending you.' And with that he breathed on them and said, 'Receive the Holy Spirit'" (John 20:21–22).

Being *sent* is not being *abandoned* to our own ideas or strength. The peace of the Spirit is a grounding presence in the life and work of the church. The Holy Spirit produces fruit and transformation of character in us (Galatians 5:22–23). The Holy Spirit accompanies us, giving the church its capacity to live into the sending that came from Jesus. The Holy Spirit provides guidance along the way. The Holy Spirit bestows gifts (Romans 12:6–8; 1 Corinthians 12–14; Ephesians 4:11–12)—the abilities we need to work within our calling. This is why Paul encouraged the church to "eagerly desire the greater gifts" and to "follow the way of love and eagerly desire gifts of the Spirit" (1 Corinthians 12:31; 14:1).

Jesus sought to live, teach, and do his work as he was directed to do so by the Father. This was an expression of *relational reliance*. The relationship between the Father and the Son is the pattern we are to practice with the Holy Spirit: we seek to live and do our work as directed by the Spirit. Following the promptings of the Holy Spirit does not set aside human thought, vision, or initiative; it means we are always delighted to bring our ideas, insights, and goals to the Spirit, asking him to give us discernment, to direct our paths, and to inspire our words and actions.

Interaction, cooperation, and friendship are the objectives here, not that we are made into robots who have no minds or feelings of our own. Actually, our work is just a pretext and context for a greater, eternal good—namely, that the character of the Spirit will increasingly become ours effortlessly and comprehensively. Dallas Willard wrote, "When our deepest attitudes and dispositions are those of Jesus, it is because we have learned to let the Spirit foster his life in us."[2] We can't participate with Jesus except through the person and work of the Holy Spirit.

If you don't know where to start in seeking a relationship with the Holy Spirit, let me guide you to Luke 11:9–13:

> "So I say to you: Ask and it will be given to you; seek and you will find; knock and the door will be opened to you. For everyone who asks receives; the one who seeks finds; and to the one who knocks, the door will be opened.
>
> "Which of you fathers, if your son asks for a fish, will give him a snake instead? Or if he asks for an egg, will give him a scorpion? If you then, though you are evil, know how to give good gifts to your children, how much more will your Father in heaven give the Holy Spirit to those who ask him!"

This delightful passage casts a vision for confident asking. Don't just be open; come to the point where you desire and ask for more of the Spirit. I ask every day, usually more than once a day. If you desire, seek, and ask, Jesus said, you will be given—you can count on it. You will notice new God-given abilities. It will be obvious that something different is animating your life. You will have fresh, instinctual love for others.

Many readers have had scary or off-putting experiences in church when it comes to the person and work of the Holy Spirit. I get it—and I empathize. Let me assure you from a lifetime of experience, you do not have to act in disconcerting or confusing ways to be filled with the Spirit. Consider this: what you saw, heard, or experienced was not the Holy Spirit per se, but the Holy Spirit within a value system, a vibe, or an ethos. But you can be free from those parameters. You can devise and live within your own value system. That is what I have done. In my best estimate, the ministry of the Holy Spirit in and through us should be expressed by:

- **Love.** When we love, we are willing the good of others, not bringing attention to ourselves.
- **Altruistic edification.** When the Spirit is at work in our lives, we will have a selfless concern for the well-being of others, seek the good of others, and never expect anything in return.
- **The Golden Rule.** When in doubt, we must never fail to do the good to others we would want done to us, and never engage in any harm to others that we would not want done to us.
- **No overacting.** The Holy Spirit will not change our tone of voice, posture, body language, or facial expressions. We just need to be ourselves. Creating hype is not helpful. What help or power could Almighty God need?
- **No manipulation.** In a community of people who are seeking to engage with the gifts of the Spirit, it is crucial that

every "word from the Lord" (wisdom, knowledge, prophecy, discerning of spirits, and the like) leaves the hearers in charge of their lives before God. If I say to someone, "I've been praying for you, and I think the Lord is saying "such and such," the receiver of the word must be in charge of discerning its legitimacy, its interpretation, and its application to their life. Gifts should never become tools for controlling others. Nor should we ever manipulate people by exaggerating claims or making false claims about one's spiritual prowess. In the life of the Spirit, we want to act with equal measures of confident faith and humility, creating and respecting space for those we interact with.

- **A sense of being naturally supernatural.** This was a favorite practice of John Wimber, founder of Vineyard Churches. The idea is that we want as much of the Spirit as he wants to give—the *supernatural*. But we want to engage with him in a way that includes the humanity of both the giver and the recipient of a gift. No putting on appearances, no striving to make an impression. Rather, we want to exercise the gifts in a spirit of humility similar to that of a postal worker or delivery person: "I am not the package and I am not the giver; I am just a conduit for the person and work of the Spirit."

- **Normal life and duty.** Not everything in life and ministry has to be exciting and provide emotional stimulation. Often this is a *fleshly energy* we can become addicted to. The animation of the Spirit has a very different feel—a sense of peace, groundedness, quiet confidence, and stability.

Don't fear the Spirit; rather, welcome the Spirit. Receive the Spirit as you would a treasured guest. Begin with a simple prayer: "Come, Holy Spirit; I welcome you to work in me and flow through me."

For our purposes in this book, it is important to note that peace is not merely an inner reality. Peace is embodied in persons and is therefore social in nature. The peace envisioned in the Bible is always meant to flow over to the good of others. A powerful and necessary creative tension exists between one's inner and relational realities. Being present to the needs of others is almost impossible when peace killers such as hurt, fear, self-defense, and soul emptiness dominate a life. That is why we rightly seek peace with God and peace within.

But seeking such peace means seeking peace in the civic dimension. A further exploration of a Spirit-filled life of justice and peace is the journey we'll take in the next chapter.

Peace with God: Since God is triune, peace with him means being at peace with the person and work of the Holy Spirit. Welcome him into your life. Eagerly desire his work in and through you. Ask for the gifts you need to be able to fulfill your calling.

Peace Within: Ask the Holy Spirit to bring the fruit of peace to your heart, soul, mind, emotions, and will. Take them one at a time, lingering a bit with each aspect as you allow the Spirit to move and speak.

Peace for the Sake of the World: Ask the Holy Spirit to make you a peacemaker. Ask for vision about to whom or to what setting you may be called. For what purpose? What exactly is the Spirit asking you to do?

CHAPTER 10

THE SPIRIT OF THE LORD'S FAVOR

Social justice concerns provide a bridge between personal ethics and social ethics.
RICHARD FOSTER, *STREAMS OF LIVING WATER*

Seemingly impossible things can be accomplished when followers of Christ deeply and imaginatively open themselves to his Spirit and follow what they understand of his revelation.
ELIZABETH O'CONNOR, *JOURNEY INWARD, JOURNEY OUTWARD*

*"The Spirit of the Lord is on me . . .
   to proclaim the year of the Lord's favor."*
LUKE 4:18–19

When our daughter, Carol, was about fourteen years old, my wife, Debbie, in her typical good wisdom, took her to see the documentary *Invisible Children*.[1] It depicts the abduction carried out by Joseph Kony and his Lord's Resistance Army (LRA) of Ugandan children who were used as child soldiers. The movie sparked a grassroots movement that galvanized and mobilized thousands of American teens and young adults into action on behalf of African children. Carol was one of them. She would not have had the vocabulary to say so, but in hindsight, it is clear that when she saw brutal, widespread evil, something was sparked in her heart that melds with "the Lord's favor" over not just the children in Uganda but also children of any race who have debilitating needs.

Most of us can recall a moment that sparked a cry in our hearts for justice and peace—for the favor of the Lord to break into the arenas of disfavor and oppression in the world. Once the spark happens, you can't unfeel it. We are beckoned to the next step on the road to justice and peace—namely, to hear a specific calling. If this call doesn't come spontaneously to you the way it did for my daughter, you can still make progress by carefully observing the world and by sitting quietly with a few questions:

- What is the meaning of *you*?
- Who are you?
- Why were you created?
- What is your place in the world?

Such questions seek one's vocation in the world. Elizabeth O'Connor wrote that vocation "has its origin in the Latin term *vocare*, to call, from which comes *vocatio*, meaning a bidding or an invitation. It implies a summoning voice which comes from above the hearer, and at the same time connects to something deep within the hearer's being."[2]

When we are wondering who we are, the first place to look is at the creation story. It tells us what God is doing and how he intends to do it in two-way companionship with his people. N. T. Wright writes about this:

> The call of the gospel is for the church to *implement* the victory of God in the world *through suffering love.* The cross is not just an example to be followed; it is an achievement to be worked out, put into practice. But it is an example, nonetheless, because it is the exemplar—the template, the model—for what God now wants to do by his Spirit in the world, through his people . . . We are to implement the achievement of Jesus and so to anticipate God's eventual [new] world.[3]

When Christians, filled and empowered by the Spirit, work to further implement the deliverance of God for the oppressed, they are cooperating, by the power of the Holy Spirit, with the inbreaking of "the Lord's favor."

That view of the church gives us a fresh way to look at sin. Sin is not just drug abuse, intolerance, conspicuous consumption, and the like. It is, as Wright says, "the rebellion of humankind against the vocation to reflect God's image into the world . . . and the loss of image-bearing humanness."[4]

When we lose consciousness of image bearing, we lose something eternally precious. Our intended destiny is to work with God forever in the new heaven and the new earth.

The words and works of Jesus form a model for Spirit engagement with the world as peacemakers. Jesus was clearly conscious of what the Father was doing in and through him:

> "The Spirit of the Lord is on me,
> because he has anointed me
> to proclaim good news to the poor.

He has sent me to proclaim freedom for the prisoners
and recovery of sight for the blind,
to set the oppressed free,
to proclaim the year of the Lord's favor."

LUKE 4:18–19

In his words and works, Jesus was self-consciously fulfilling the messianic prophecy of Isaiah (61:1–2). The prophetic tradition describes the focus and tenor of his ministry. "The year of the Lord's favor" points to the fact that Jesus' effect on the world was a type of "jubilee" (Leviticus 25:8–13). The jubilee set people free from their debts, liberated all slaves, and returned property to those who had previously owned it. It was a whole-life, whole-community reset. It was a massive act of justice. It was an act of healing for the emotional, social, and spiritual ills of God's people. It was the gift of personal liberty that was intended to give the great gift of "the simple life," which in turn brought rest—and the peace, freedom, and justice that flow from it.

Jesus ushered into being the time of God's extraordinary kindness—release, relief, respite. People could take a break, take a breath, enjoy a fresh start, a new beginning in him. Can you feel the *favor* to which Jesus pointed—the mix of freedom and peace, of rest and contentment, of reset and sighs of relief? This is the fusion of inner peace and missional action imparted to us in the sending of Jesus and the Spirit.

Jesus knew that for full-orbed peace to come, things would have to change. He had to confront the powers—personal, communal, and governmental. Jesus also had in his sights the spiritual principalities and powers (Colossians 2:15; Ephesians 3:10; 6:12) that typically undergird human evil and injustice. In a sense, Jesus was an activist. As Obery Hendricks Jr. wrote, "For him [Jesus] true spirituality consisted of an active commitment to health, wholeness, and justice for all God's children as the highest expression of our love for God."[5]

Jesus had a concrete, contemporary context in mind as he read the ancient words of Isaiah. The "year of the Lord's favor" implied changing, not conserving or protecting, what existed:

- Jails were full of economically exploited people who, through no fault of their own, could not pay back their debts; these people could expect release.
- Those who felt every aspect of their lives crushed under the oppression of the Roman Empire would see the light of freedom at the end of the tunnel.
- The poor, who were made that way by unjust taxes, could foresee deliverance.
- Religious oppression from the misguided priestly class, often in cahoots with Rome, would come to an end.
- Jewish people may have heard in Jesus' words an echo of the miracle of the exodus, and may have found the hope for a new exodus led by a new and better Moses—namely, Jesus.
- With the coming of Jesus, and with the final coming of God's new world, various manifestations of the status quo would be dismissed in favor of "your kingdom come, your will be done" (Matthew 6:10).

As we concentrate on the overall work of the Spirit of peace, it is important to note that Jesus claims to be operating in the power of the Holy Spirit: "The Spirit of the Lord is on me" (Luke 4:18). At his baptism, "the Holy Spirit descended on him in bodily form like a dove" (3:22). Next, Luke tells us that "Jesus, full of the Holy Spirit, left the Jordan and was led by the Spirit into the wilderness" (4:1). When the narrative shifts to our passage

(4:18–19), Luke describes the way Jesus came back into the public eye, launching his ministry in Galilee "in the power of the Spirit" (v. 14). As we receive and interact with the Holy Spirit, we obtain both his peace and his sentness into the world to work with Jesus in bringing favor to the world.

This means the Spirit was and is active in proclaiming good news to the poor, freeing prisoners, healing the blind, setting the oppressed free, and bringing to bear the time of the Lord's favor. We see the Jesus-Spirit connection clearly when Peter explains the Jesus movement to Cornelius:

> "You know the message God sent to the people of Israel, announcing the good news of peace through Jesus Christ, who is Lord of all . . . [and] how God anointed Jesus of Nazareth with the Holy Spirit and power, and how he went around doing good and healing all who were under the power of the devil, because God was with him."
>
> ACTS 10:36, 38

Peter was aware of two things: (1) Jesus meant to bring holistic salvation to the world—forgiving sins, healing, freeing, delivering justice to the downtrodden; and (2) Jesus' activities of peace and justice were occurring by means of his anointing by the Spirit. When Jesus drove out demons, deep peace was the effect. When he told the Pharisees, "You load people down with burdens they can hardly carry, and you yourselves will not lift one finger to help them" (Luke 11:46), he demonstrated that he was inducing a religious exodus of sorts. When he raised the dead, he signaled the eternal reality of "the Lord's favor." When he speaks to outsiders—women, Samaritans, tax collectors, and various kinds of sinners—he signals the relational peace that humans were meant to enjoy.

My colleague Esau McCaulley makes clear the holism Jesus pursued:

> Jesus' ministry and the kingdom that he embodies involves nothing less than the creation of a new world in which the marginalized are healed spiritually, economically, and psychologically. The wealthy, inasmuch as they participate in and adopt the values of a society that dehumanizes people, find themselves opposing the reign of God. This dehumanization can take two forms. First, it can treat the poor as mere bodies that need food and not the transforming love of God. Second, it can view them as souls whose experience of the here and now should not trouble us. This a false religion that has little to do with Jesus.[6]

The same Spirit who was with Jesus in his ministry to the poor, the imprisoned, the sick, and the oppressed is with us, at work in the world to empower our works of mercy and justice. The Spirit enables our active role as *peacemakers* in our immediate contexts. The gifts of the Spirit (discernment, wisdom, knowledge, prophecy, and the like) alert the church to where God is at work in the world, prompting the church to join him there. The Spirit has a mission too, not just Jesus. The Spirit is focused on the full accomplishment of that which the Father was doing in Jesus to call and send a people into the world as *workers of his will*. Salvation—deliverance, healing, justice, freedom for the oppressed, the bringing of creation to its magnificent intended completion—is a Trinitarian effort, with all three members at work. Our age is the age of the Spirit. He assists us and empowers us to be faithful to God's will, both for the church and in the world.

The church that seeks justice *and* peace desires and welcomes the Spirit to be *within* us in peace and *on* us in power to serve others. The cross and resurrection are, appropriately so, the central focus of the Christian life, but we ignore Pentecost at great cost. The "year of the Lord's favor," as carried out by the church, is a work of the Holy Spirit. *Anointing* should not be thought of as an obscure Pentecostal or charismatic term. Being anointed by the Spirit is ground zero for the life of the church in the world.

The Spirit of peace is also the Spirit of the body of Christ in action. Eugene Schlesinger writes, "There is, then, an inseparable unity between Christ and his body, the church. Together, they form one person, which is bound together by the Holy Spirit, who animates the body of Christ."[7] The promise that the Spirit will "be with you forever" (John 14:16) is meant both to cure anxiety (the disciples were fearful because Jesus had just announced his departure) and to give peace in mission, the peace of being companioned in the hard work of justice and peacemaking.

Face It

Institutional and structural injustice is overwhelming to me. I wonder if the feeling of being overpowered and outmatched by evil is part of what has made focusing on injustice hard for me. Facing this part of transformation into Christlikeness is crucial, for "co-creation is the essence of our vocation . . . [and precipitates] an engagement with dark forces churning within [us]."[8] In fact, "one of the ways we know a call to be God's call is when a feeling of awe-filled dread is combined with one of being companioned."[9] Maybe you feel overwhelmed by injustice as well? If so, like me, maybe you will be helped by the insights of Henri Nouwen and Richard Foster:

> They [Christian leaders] have to say "no" to every form
> of fatalism, defeatism, accidentalism or incidentalism which

make people believe that statistics are telling us the truth. They have to say "no" to every form of despair in which human life is seen as a pure matter of good or bad luck. They have to say "no" to sentimental attempts to make people develop a spirit of resignation or stoic indifference in the face of the unavoidability of pain, suffering, and death.[10]

Now, the battlefronts [of justice] in the institutional arena are myriad, and some of them are terribly complicated, for they become all tangled up in historical allegiances and cultural traditions and political interests. *But face them we must.* The plight of the unborn. Problems of poverty and housing. Issues of nationalism and militarism. Of war and peace. Of racism. Of sexism. Of ageism. Of consumerism. Of environmentalism.[11]

Should I Be a Charismatic?

If by being charismatic, one means participating in certain forms of worship services, then no, you don't need to become a charismatic. But if by charismatic one means the experience of the *charismata* (the Greek word for "gifts" in Romans 12 and 1 Corinthians 12), then the answer is yes—please become one now! The biblical expectation is that followers of Jesus will regularly receive capacities from the Spirit that assist their formation in peace, facilitate the healing and edification of the faith community, and empower their mission and justice-seeking in the world.

Yet our lives, as Elizabeth O'Connor reminded us, are often "like frozen ponds where everything fiery in us has been put on ice."[12] The church must reverse this reality, for it cannot be energized in the direction of peacemaking by personal guilt and shame. There is one source of power for living a life that is in tune with the Lord's favor—namely, the person and work of the Holy

Spirit. The Spirit gives the ability to reflect on and respond to the issues of life with the intentionality of Jesus, bringing the Lord's favor to bear on broken humanity. With God at the center of our lives, we then see the world differently. We feel human pain and experience divine hope.

How to Begin as a Peace-Filled Peacemaker

Right, you may be thinking, *but how do I begin?* You begin by looking *within* and *without*.

Looking within is a common strategy for hearing the voice of the Spirit. Two of my most trusted guides give insight here. Gordon Cosby once said, "It is the faith that God has called us— each of us—into being to play a part in His cosmic drama . . . Hints of what this part is come to us through our deepest longings and desires. What we deeply want to do is often what we ought to do. What we think we *ought* to do and feel compelled to do may not be God's intention at all."[13] Elizabeth O'Connor helps us see what happens when we try to work outside of our true passion: "Out of touch with the life-giving energy of our wants and desires, we are . . . apt to become flat and uninteresting people."[14] Think about how you would answer this question: *What would I do if I could?* Then seek the power of the Spirit to do it.

Look outward as another way to find a starting place. This process is helped along by a different set of reflections: *What in the people and events of the world causes me pain? What breaks my heart and makes me cry? What, if it were to be healed or fixed, would bring great joy?* Earlier I told you the story of our daughter, Carol—for her the answer to each of these questions revolved around children. For my wife, Debbie, it was all the aspects of pain that surround abortion. Where do you catch a glimpse of a better world? Whatever that is, it may be your calling.

Noticing our empathetic pain and hearing a calling to get involved with it, plus receiving the gifts invoked by this calling, lead, even while ministering in situations of deep pain, to being "at play in the world . . . Hope begins to grow, and we are summoned to the work that will give us a feeling of wellness and make possible that which we envision."[15]

Jesus and Politics

If you are afraid that focusing on justice, mercy, and "the year of the Lord's favor" is introducing politics into religion, you can relax. The Jesus movement as described above is unavoidably political in the sense that it affects the way humans order themselves in society. But it doesn't mean we have to engage in the current bitter, brutal, partisan political wars. *What the Bible has in view transcends liberal Democrats and conservative Republicans.* The Spirit-impassioned work to which followers of Jesus are called means this:

> We Christians must not let ourselves be deceived into either exclusive allegiance or exclusive opposition to either party. What must be opposed is valorization of the rich as if they have a natural right to rule. What must be opposed is moral laxity masquerading as liberation. What must be opposed is hunger and violence and exploitation and oppression, and mistreatment of anyone for any reason. We must oppose all these because they fly in the face of the politics of Jesus. To do otherwise is to dishonor his ministry, his mission, and the death he willingly died for our sakes.[16]

Jesus started a movement of salvation that is best understood in the most comprehensive terms one can imagine—in the phrase *new creation*. The Jesus movement is inward and outward, spiritual and material, hidden and public, religious and political. It is a movement toward eternal peace in a renewed creation.

The Jesus movement issues a summons to a holy calling and grants a great privilege to those who hear and follow him in the establishment of God's kingdom of love, righteousness, and justice. Jesus knew his words and actions didn't occur in a religious bubble but within warring kingdoms—darkness and evil versus light and justice. He declared, given the reality of spiritual warfare, "Whoever is not with me is against me" (Matthew 12:30).

I'll bet, like me, you want to be with him.

Deep peace is peace that works its way to the center of our being—heart, soul, mind, emotions, and will. In the next section, we will focus on finding the inward peace necessary to become outward peacemakers, to bring justice and peace to our everyday lives.

Peace with God: Because Jesus said, "Come, follow me," participating in "the year of the Lord's favor" places a claim on our lives. How do you feel about this? Is it a new thought? If so, how are you responding? Is it a source of tension between you and God? If so, see if you can name the source of the tension and talk about it with God.

Peace Within: Are there areas of your life that remain untouched by "the year of the Lord's favor"? Specify them and consider them. Have you been hiding them? Have you been unaware of them? Once you can identify them, welcome the Spirit into your life to bring healing and freedom.

Peace for the Sake of the World: If your walk with Christ has been marked mostly by inner work, how can you leverage the best parts of your spiritual growth for the sake of others? Consider saying yes to a call that will invoke *new* gifts in you.

PEACE WITHIN

CHAPTER 11

CULTIVATING A MELLOW HEART

*The gifts of simplicity and a life defined by
humble alignment to God are a quiet mind, a
peaceful heart, and a settled soul.*

We've all known people who are hyperreactive. How many times have we said things like, "Don't bring up SEC football with Uncle Tim!" or "Please don't talk about liberal politics with Aunt Jayne!" Everyone in the family knows that, with the slightest prodding, these folks pop like a balloon, spreading nasty remarks all over the room. This sort of anxiety pushes strongly against consistent peace. The opposite of peace is not merely conflict or war, but also anxiety marked by a noisy mind and an irritated soul.

Peace is not merely an absence—such as the absence of war or relational conflicts of various sorts. It is the positive experience of the presence of something that feels strong and steadfast. Peace is a character trait, a grounding virtue—an inner readiness or disposition to act in peace. It is an everyday, ordinary manner of being. It gives our inner being the sense of wholeness and structural integrity among our many *parts*—heart, mind, emotions, body, soul, and social setting.

Jesus came to bring just such peace. He came "to shine on those living in darkness and in the shadow of death, to guide our feet into the path of peace" (Luke 1:79). At Jesus' birth, the heavenly hosts exclaimed, "Glory to God in the highest heaven, and on earth peace to those on whom his favor rests" (Luke 2:14). At the end of Jesus' earthly ministry, he said to a confused and conflicted group of disciples, "Peace be with you" (Luke 24:36). Peace is core to Jesus' person and central to his work in the church and the world.

Wait a minute! Didn't Jesus also say he came to bring a sword and to bring division? Didn't he say nasty things to religious leaders? Take these few statements, for example:

> "Do not suppose that I have come to bring peace to the earth. I did not come to bring peace, but a sword" (Matthew 10:34).
> "Do you think I came to bring peace on earth? No, I tell you, but division" (Luke 12:51).
> "Woe to you . . . you hypocrites! . . . blind guides! . . . You snakes! You brood of vipers! How will you escape being condemned to hell?" (Matthew 23:15–16, 33)

Isn't that a picture of the robust, fierce Jesus? As a practical matter, isn't *peace* a weak delusion? What are we supposed to make of these Scriptures? How can they possibly fit with the image of the Prince of Peace (Isaiah 9:6) who came to give peace (John 14:27)? What's more, what about Paul's exhortation to let the peace of Christ rule in our hearts (Colossians 3:15)?

The peace that Jesus brought with him was not a universal, immediate peace. Neither was it the kind that comes on the heels of victory in a war or through a process of political compromise.

Jesus' peace was a picture of the nature of God. The biblical vision is that such peace will saturate the hearts of his followers and lead to the healing and deliverance of others. All sword-swinging separation happens under the overall canopy of God's love, wisdom, grace, and peace. Any swinging of swords we resort to when we lack the whole truth is usually angry, wild, imprecise, and unfair. A friend of mine used to say, "I trust Jesus' anger; I'm just not so sure about yours!"

The division that Jesus speaks of is created by decisions—of belief or unbelief, transformation of the old self or a clinging to it; hypocrisy and superstition or genuine spirituality; pride and lust or humility and self-sacrifice. Whenever a bright light is turned on, it divides the darkness from the light. There are unavoidable consequences as the unseen now becomes seen. Some run from the light in the fear that it will expose things they prefer to stay hidden. Others delight in the light.

I've had powerful and unpleasant experiences with this. In the 1970s I worked for the city of Anaheim at Anaheim Stadium (the "Big A"). It primarily meant working during the baseball games of the California Angels, but there were occasional rock concerts. During these concerts, most of the lights would be off so attention could be focused on the concert stage. Once the concert ended, the lights would come on so the crowd could file out safely. You do not want me to describe the ugly, nauseating mess the light revealed. The light first brought *reality*, but the light also served to assist the cleaning team as they put the Big A back in shape.

Someday the cosmic lights will come on. In that moment, God will "reconcile to himself all things, whether things on earth or things in heaven, by making *peace* through his blood, shed on the cross" (Colossians 1:20, emphasis mine). The person and death of Jesus are what assure this cosmic, eternal peace: "For he himself is our peace . . . His purpose was to create in himself one new humanity out of the two, thus making peace . . . He came and preached peace to you who were far away and peace to those who were near" (Ephesians 2:14–15, 17).

The prophet Isaiah brings into focus God's intent to bring peace at the coming of the Messiah: "You will keep the man in perfect peace whose mind is kept on You, because he trusts in You" (Isaiah 26:3 NLV). He envisions a day when "all your children will be taught by the LORD, and great will be their peace" (54:13), and when we will hear the Lord say, "Peace, peace, to those far and near" (57:19). Isaiah foretells the day when God will extend "peace . . . like a river" (66:12) and when God's people "will live in peaceful dwelling places, in secure homes, in undisturbed places of rest" (32:18).

How can we describe a heart alive with the vision of Isaiah? I like a word that may surprise some of us—the word *mellow*.

A Mellow Heart

As I prepared to write this book, a friend gave me a book about gentleness that caught my attention with the author's use of the word *mellow*.[1] I've read many books about Christian spirituality, but I've never seen *mellow* used in that genre. A *mellow* heart[2]— now that's an arresting thought. The term *mellow* brings me back to my 1970s adolescence. "Mellow out, dude!" It's similar to today's "Chill out!" and "Lighten up!"

Is being mellow a valid virtue to be pursued in Christian spirituality? I believe it is. It's a powerful image for both the way we pursue formation in Christlikeness and the outcome we aim for as disciples of Jesus.

The word *mellow* suggests an evolution from a previous anxious or uptight state. It has the connotation of smooth—as in not harsh, biting, or rough. It suggests being soft and tender in our approach rather than rigid and difficult. It alludes to a ripeness or maturity that bypasses immature approaches to life. It calls to mind being levelheaded and settled in contrast to being hotheaded and impulsive. I've thought a lot now about a mellow heart or spirit, and I see this surprising word as both the attitude with which we seek to follow Jesus and the outcome of doing so. We will do well to seek a mellow heart, little by little every day, as the sure pathway to peace. Without it, we will surely find ourselves in bondage to the forces of darkness.

Polarization and Animosity

Polarization and animosity are now valued, cultivated, and rationalized by clicks and profits, by gaining power, by getting votes. But peace that comes from adopting the way of Jesus represents a better way to achieve important goals.

The secular government of Rome and the major Jewish sects (the politically oriented Herodians, the escapist Essenes of the Qumran community, and the war-focused Zealots) would have known that Jesus was articulating an alternative worldview and a different way of living. Jesus wasn't shy about what he taught, but he never let himself get polarized in the ways that dominate our contemporary social discourse.

Too often we have lost the ability to do life without placing on others easy labels—ones that are usually incomplete if not flat-out wrong. This behavior is an enemy of peace. Sadly, it occupies a large part of our inner life and drives our habitual interior dialogue. Those we have labeled become our conversation partners in daydreams where we imagine slaying someone with our verbal retorts. Dream these things enough, and they come to pass in our everyday lives. Far too many people think that being *oppositional*, *antagonistic*, and *contradictory* is to be valued above all else these days. Social media is all the proof we need. Check the movies that play in your head. Are you typically the hero who verbally defeats the bad guys? Why do you think this is? What are you getting out of it? How is it going for you? Are you tired of having an estranged family and few friends? Or is it worth it to you?

As Jesus took on what seemed to be unmovable forces of sin, pain, and injustice, he was not adversarial. He wasn't constantly looking for an argument. He didn't go around searching for new foes so he could use them to position himself on a given spectrum that was created by humans. Jesus defined himself not on the basis of others but on this basis: "I have come down from heaven not to do my will but to do the will of him who sent me" (John 6:38). He was seeking to obey his Father and to draw followers who would follow his way along the way. He was happy to point out that which was misaligned to his work—in the Jewish religious leaders, in his disciples, in onlookers to his ministry, in society. But Jesus' observations always were delivered in a way that gave space to others to have their own lives before God—for now. Someday God will insist on his will—and there will be no arguing.

Jesus' disciples were at least as smart as we are. They understood their lives in a manner similar to you and me. Our technologies for knowing may be different, and the scope of knowledge much greater today, but they understood life as it presented itself to them. And because of that understanding, they knew they had the option of choosing violent political stances. Yet for the most part, adopting the characteristics of Jesus, they did not do so. They chose to emulate Jesus—to act justly with grace, patience, love, service, and peace.

We can't do those things with a nervous, restless soul. In the next chapter, we will uncover some practical ways to develop a nonanxious soul.

Peace with God: In illustrating an important aspect of peace with God, Jesus said, "I have come down from heaven not to do my will but to do the will of him who sent me" (John 6:38). Does this sort of vow reside in you? Why or why not?

Peace Within: This chapter speaks of a "mellow heart." Is this a positive and appealing quality to you? What works against it in your life? What can you do to work toward it?

Peace for the Sake of the World: The New Testament priest Zechariah told us that Jesus came "to guide our feet into the path of peace" (Luke 1:79). As one of Jesus' cooperative friends, can you think of situations in which you can be a peacemaker and guide people into the path of peace?

CHAPTER 12

WHY SO ANXIOUS, O MY SOUL?

Never be in a hurry; do everything quietly and
in a calm spirit. Do not lose your inner peace
for anything whatsoever, even if your whole
world seems upset.

FRANCIS DE SALES

Driving home from work, the adrenaline of the day fading away, I rolled down the car window to let in some refreshing spring air. I expected the breeze to carry peace. But as I sat at the traffic light, my shoulders lifted toward my ears, then back toward the seat, and then down again. I moved each one—left, then right. Definitely some tightness there. Opening and closing my mouth, I noticed a slight ache in my jaw. The high-energy, nonstop activity of the day had also masked a dull headache I was now feeling. The light turned green, and I asked myself, *What the heck is wrong with me? Where is all this embodied stress coming from?*

Why is peace elusive? Because there are so many reasons for anxiety. Our minds often race with negative thoughts. Bad memories and bad dreams produce disquiet. There are fractured relationships in our families, at work, or at school. Money problems and struggling marriages are common. Our political system is marked by hateful division. Nations war with each other. We get sick. People we love get seriously sick. Friends and relatives die.

Over many years of listening to people as a pastor, leader, professor, and public speaker, I have heard countless men and women, young and old, describe themselves by saying, "My anxiety sometimes takes center stage in my life. It is overwhelming. Occasionally I can think of nothing else. No coping mechanism seems to work. I need to know: How can I find peace within?"

Anxiety may be in our face, but it does not have to rule over us. We can change the way we face it. We want to come to the place where we relate to the people and events of our lives in peace, without, as Adrian van Kaam wrote, the "compulsion to be more efficient, more clever or faster than I reasonably could be in a relaxed manner . . . [We want to do life] without the eagerness to hurry up the process . . . [And we want] to let the spirit of gentility [and peace] invade our work."[1]

Jesus said, "Peace I leave with you; my peace I give you. I do not give to you as the world gives. Do not let your hearts be troubled and do not be afraid" (John 14:27). Jesus explains that the peace he gives is *his*. It is the peace he himself experienced. This peace is very different from the shallow, temporary peace that may result from the various distractions and medications of the world. In contrast, Jesus wanted the church to have his rich and full peace that would overflow to others.

This peace is experienced when we come to realize we have nothing to defend, protect, or seize. Everything we need has been given to us. We don't have to live in the fearful worry of *lack*.[2] Different drivers of the heart are possible.

A Nonanxious Inner Life

Jesus was pointing to a particular inner life when he said, "Come to me, all you who are weary and burdened, and I will give you rest. Take my yoke upon you and learn from me, for I am gentle and humble in heart, and you will find rest for your souls. For my yoke is easy and my burden is light" (Matthew 11:28–30).

Rest. Anxiety produces busyness, and a hectic life produces uneasiness. Around and around this reality goes in a vicious cycle of inner conflict. We are driven to produce goods or provide services and to make money. We are preoccupied with achievement. We are absorbed in managing our image.

Anxious people can rarely cease their nervous commotion or simply sit still. Something is always wrong, or *could* go wrong. Such things need to be fixed or headed off. Now! For the really anxious, sleep can be a hoped-for but rare feat. We lack the patience to discover and deal with the underlying issue or issues. There are always pills to take or beverages to drink that may bring short-term pseudo-relief.

A life of rest doesn't mean we never work hard. Rather, Jesus is inviting us to cease striving. Working and striving are very different things. When I write, teach, or coach others, I feel calm and at ease and the time flies as ideas and words come to me. But I agonize over other elements of life. In rest, Jesus invites us to pause and recover from life's strenuousness and receive a quiet mind and a calm heart.

Rest is not just the brief break we take to catch our breath in the middle of our physical work. Envisioned in Jesus' invitation is a person fundamentally at rest in the midst of daily and, yes, occasionally challenging work. The vision is that in Christ our rest is not just an intermission between stretches of work, but true rejuvenation, renewal, restoration, refreshment, and replenishing.

In place of the word *rest*, William Tyndale's early translation of the Bible has Jesus saying, "I will *ease* you." The idea is that we are *relieved*. Relieved from the duty we have felt to remain in charge and alleviate the pain and disorientation caused by the stressors of life. To be at ease includes being rescued from trouble, bother, and difficulty—the nervous, uptight way we do life. Those at ease still do good work—a lot of it. But they move at a new, graceful pace. A renovated state of heart and mind is theirs in Christ, which brings freedom and release from struggling over the people and events of their lives. To be at peace is to be at ease.

A new yoke. Jesus' hearers would have understood the word *yoke* to refer to bondage or slavery. A passage in Leviticus gives a window through which to see this: "I am the LORD your God, who brought you out of Egypt so that you would no longer be slaves to the Egyptians; I broke the bars of your yoke and enabled you to walk with heads held high" (Leviticus 26:13).

Jesus' hearers might also have thought of the yoke of fastidious legal observance that was modeled by and heaped on people by the teachers of the law and the Pharisees. Jesus said, "And you experts in the law, woe to you, because you load people down with burdens they can hardly carry, and you yourselves will not lift one finger to help them" (Luke 11:46).

Jesus was entirely different—in orientation, attitude, word, and action—from the religious leaders of his day. Jesus perfectly fulfilled the law (Matthew 5:17) in a way that others experienced as for their good. Yet in that religious or spiritual perfection, he was not an oppressive load to be carried. Rather, Jesus was the chief initiator, actor, and energy within the yoke. He carried the heavy load in service to others.

Being yoked with Jesus implies a close relationship of walking together, in this case as a teacher with his students in kingdom living. It also refers to the manner in which Jesus defeated bondage, slavery, and corrupt religion. Jesus' yoke is colored with peace, with joyful obedience, with heartfelt and eager submission to the purposes and plans of his Father. Jesus did not feed on inner angst as motivation or rely on conflict to get his way. Presence, not power, was his mode of being. Love, not the need to control, marked his relational ethic.

There is a great irony to being yoked with Jesus. When I imagine putting my head into the hoop of a yoke, I feel bound, constricted, even claustrophobic. The paradox is that outside of Jesus' yoke, I am tightly bound to habits of sin, but inside his yoke I find partnership, healing, and freedom: "Very truly I tell you, everyone who sins is a slave to sin . . . [But] if the Son sets you free, you will be free indeed" (John 8:34, 36).

Thus, the fear we may have of yielding everything, as the hoop of the yoke suggests, is a deceit—no matter how strongly we may feel the fear. In actuality, being yoked with Jesus is to have a new, powerfully effective assist for doing life. The hoop that invites our head is the place of restriction, yet it is also the source of relief, like a ring tossed to someone drowning. It stills the panic of life.

But being in a yoke with Jesus does not mean ceasing all activity. A yoke is precisely a tool for doing work. There is labor to be done, acts of service to be carried out, life to be lived. But this yoke of Jesus, and the effort we exert with it on, is *easy*—it is "fit," "manageable," "kind," "benevolent."[3]

- *Fit*—rather than taking us outside ourselves into unhealthy work, the yoke of Jesus takes into account and facilitates the fact that our work is done out of the overflow of our total being—passions, spiritual gifts, and temperament.
- *Manageable*—the yoke of Jesus does not require over-the-top levels of activity, just modest days of work in which we yield outcomes to God.
- *Kind*—being yoked with Jesus means we never need to be

rude, inconsiderate, or cruel in order to live into our passions, pursue our visions, or do our work.

- *Benevolent*—the inclination to be kind, to live out of the well of tenderhearted love, is deep in the very grain of the wood from which the yoke of Jesus is made; yoked with Jesus, we never need to protect ourselves through tightfisted, stingy greed in which the people and events of our lives are used for our own grasping, selfish purposes.

We tend to think that virtue, character, religious morals, and spirituality are simply about self-restraint. Certainly, curbing our bad actions or regulating our harsh words is better than, for instance, stealing or cussing someone out. But subjecting ourselves to religious laws and battling our truest desires by means of mere self-restrictions are not healthy long-term spiritual strategies. This approach to the spiritual life puts a new and different yoke on us—a heavy one, one marked by self-salvation and self-transformation. Such a yoke cannot generate the life of Jesus within us. It cannot produce natural actions of love and peace, among others. Jesus wants us to have a different sort of religious life—namely, one that is in him, with him, through him.

A light burden. Most people surmise that religion is a burden, that it puts something unnatural on us. It tries to force us to do things we don't really want to do. Religion seeks to make us stop things we seem to completely desire. This creates a great riddle: Isn't there something virtuous about being one's truest self? Yes, but *true* does not mean *good*. *Intuitive* or *instinctual* may or may not imply *suitable* or *appropriate*. The fact is that often our truest selves need repentance and change.

For example, it can seem totally natural not to pay invoices owed to vendors, using them as unwilling lines of credit. *After all*, we think, *I need to stay in business.* We commonly and easily rationalize the need to lie in order to protect ourselves or manage our image. If we are lonely and needy enough, it can seem perfectly appropriate to engage in the sex that we believe will take our attention off our pain for a while. Our inner life, our self-talk (until it takes on a Jesus shape), cannot be relied on. In the words of the prophet Jeremiah, "The heart is deceitful above all things and beyond cure. Who can understand it?" (17:9).

Jesus is inviting us into a relational reality in which life is lived in a transformed way. We are called to set aside the fight against our disordered desires in favor of cultivating the aspiration to do good to others. We begin to nurture genuine confidence and trust in God so that we don't feel the fear-based need to lie and therefore can tell the truth. We seek to be so nourished in our inner being that we never need to sexually use others to heal our pain. Transformation into Christlikeness, with its attendant peace, is the good life—it is the light burden. Jesus stands before you with an invitation: lay down the inferior, enslaved ways of being human and pick up a new life in him as his follower, learning to live your life as he would if he were in your place. If you can imagine this, you have a sufficient imagination for good religion, for freedom, for love, for peace.

You Don't Need Your Anxiety

Some of us have come to accept that "I'm just an anxious person by nature." We have also learned to use the fear and dread we feel to motivate action, especially actions we would rather put off. We've made friends with our anxiety for utilitarian purposes. We've made a deal with anxiety, saying, "Don't get to the point where you're debilitating, and I won't send you packing."

But here's the truth: anything that can be done through the impulse of anxiety can be done better without it. Anxiety pollutes. Relationally, it is an unattractive quality. It unpleasantly taints our work. Our creativity suffers. Anxiety makes us driven more than it makes us passionate.

Don't worry, peace doesn't mean we are so relaxed or laissez-faire that we always give in, seek to keep the peace at all costs, or never get anything worthwhile done. Peaceful people get good work done, achieve new heights in their fields, make great contributions to humanity, and make strong and principled stands—as did Jesus. But they do so with different motivations and by different practices and they achieve different, more holistic outcomes.

Different motivations. If you have a passion for children, you can't be blamed for feeling alarmed when you see images or hear stories of their mistreatment or abandonment. If you feel called to fight against racial injustice, it is natural for you to recoil in horror at racist behaviors. The occasional, spontaneous intrusion of anxious feelings is common. But these feelings are not your boss. Your guiding light is the good you wish to do, based on your calling and gifts. Our life's work can come from peace. It can flow from a gentle, settled confidence in God. Instead of anxiety, the assurance of our calling and a childlike dependence on the gifts of the Holy Spirit can be the drivers of the good we wish to do in the world.

Different practices. Practices are not neutral, nor do they arise out of the blue. For instance, anxiety has various experiences associated with it—hurry, impatience, avoidance of challenging people or difficult decisions, a pessimistic view of life, feelings of helplessness or hopelessness, a tendency to see danger when there is none, a sense of alienation from others. These feelings and experiences then lead to practices such as cutting corners, cutting people off, canceling meetings, putting off challenging but necessary conversations, fudging the truth on reports, hiding or isolating, and causing division.

Practices that flow from and make for peace are much different. Peaceful people are able to be fully present; being at peace, they have good focus and are capable of taking on and completing their work. Because their poise is rooted in their relationship with God, they feel no need to misrepresent reality. They have the ability to stay connected in peaceful ways to perplexing decisions and problematic people.

Different outcomes. The outcomes that flow from peace have certain characteristics. When people see them, they realize that something different is at play here. The vibe, ethos, and culture feel different. Instead of separating into winners and losers, people are aligned, no matter what their background or giftedness, with a common vision. Outcomes birthed in peace are God-honoring. They result in long-term, long-lasting fruitfulness. They create spaces of peace. They achieve the most good for the widest possible group of people.

A common misunderstanding is that in order to do good things we need to force things to happen. It doesn't work. Have you ever tried to force yourself to fall asleep or to stay calm—no way! If you've ever tried golfing, painting, dancing, or hunting, you know you can't force it. You can only work yourself gently and persistently toward proficiency. Strong self-assertion disconnected from the work of God is a peace stealer. Gaining peace is more a matter of receptivity than force. As you seek peace, maintain a sense of playfulness and lightheartedness about it, being mindful and thoughtful but not too stern or serious. The pursuit of godly outcomes must leave room for exploration and spontaneity. We want to practice our growth *toward* peace *in* peace.

Tangible Peace

Peace is acquired not in abstractions but in real life—among people with names and in concrete situations. These are the only places where peace is passed on as well. This means we must be courageously connected to reality. Everyone will lose their peace from time to time. That's fine, but if you catch yourself in the grips of anxiety, then pivot and employ the spiritual practices that lead to peace.

Learning to pivot or repent in the moment is central to being a student of Jesus. Dallas Willard wrote that Jesus is leading "a revolution of character, which proceeds by changing people from the inside through ongoing personal relationship to God in Christ and to one another. It is one that changes their ideas, beliefs, feelings, and habits of choice, as well as their bodily tendencies and social relations. It penetrates to the deepest layers of their soul."[4]

If you struggle with anxiety, consider this: you are more than your current emotional state. You have thoughts and a will. You have a vision for becoming a person of peace. Nourish yourself with peaceful thoughts, images, and ideas. Music works well for me. Before work, on my home from work, or in the middle of my day, I often sit still and meditate on songs like "A Cloud of Peace,"[5] "Be Still,"[6] "Grace and Peace,"[7] or some version of "It Is Well with My Soul" or "Be Thou My Vision."[8] Increasingly, I create or borrow and make use of breath prayers.[9] I practice times of silence and solitude. I go for a gentle, reflective walk. Playing the piano takes me to a different inner space. Reading authors who write about peace provides me with models of the life I seek and gives me hope to pursue it.

Practices like these—or ones you select or create yourself—provide a wider view of reality. They push anxiety back, untwisting it from your heart, loosening its deforming grip on your mind. We need these spiritual inputs to put anxious thoughts in their place, making them seem less overwhelming. The practices I've just cited as examples create new habits of the heart, mind, will, and emotions, thereby providing small but stable stepping-stones on the path to peace.

For many of us, the biggest battle for peace has to do with our mind. It can seem out of control with self-accusation, false think-ing, habitual judgment of others, and complaints about God. We are more than just our mind, but the mind can be either an ally or an enemy in our quest for peace. In the next chapter, we'll take a look at the intersection of our mind and peace.

Peace with God: Think back on a few lovely and powerful words of Scripture: "My peace I [Jesus] give you" (John 14:27); "You will find rest for your souls" (Matthew 11:29); "If the Son sets you free, you will be free indeed" (John 8:36). In what aspects of your life do you feel these things? Where are they noticeably absent? What can you learn from your assessment?

Peace Within: Given our typical anxieties, what do you think or feel about Jesus' invitation to take on his yoke—his light burden? What would have to change for you to pull yourself close enough to Jesus to be yoked with him?

Peace for the Sake of the World: Can you identify how the overflow of your anxiety harms others? If you can see it, fearlessly name it, and ask for forgiveness and correc-tion, you will take a big step toward being at peace for the sake of the important relationships in your life.

CHAPTER 13

PEACE FOR AN ANXIOUS MIND

*The silence holds with its gloved hand the wild
hawk of the mind.*

R. S. THOMAS, "THE UNTAMED"

*The mind governed by the flesh is death, but
the mind governed by the Spirit is life and
peace.*

ROMANS 8:6

Mason had looked forward to seeing Lilly all week. She was
coming into town for a work-related conference. She had
Friday evening off before needing to catch an early morning flight
home on Saturday. Studying economics at university, Mason and
Lilly had become heart-sharing friends. Intellectual conversations about the subtle intricacies of the global economy frequently
turned to their various personal concerns.

They worried out loud to each other about their fears—which
usually had to do with financial or political uncertainties. As
they sat down for dinner, alternating between looking at the

menu and at each other, they caught up, exchanging their usual chitchat. Once the waiter took their order, Mason, ready to get a robust conversation going, dove in:

> My God, Lilly! This mind of mine—what am I going to do with it? I drive myself crazy with anxiety by the false stories I tell myself. Sometimes I make arrogant mental projections about future successes in my publishing or about climbing the ladder at the university. Other times I play and replay fearful tapes that convince me I have no respectable academic future at all. And if these two patterns aren't harassing me, my thoughts can get stuck in an endless cycle of imagining what others think of me.

Lilly, feeling the familiar warm comfort of her friend, quickly jumped in:

> I so get it! My mind is constantly calculating, analyzing, estimating, anticipating, and projecting itself into the future. I'm always waiting for some imagined prospect to arrive. Some days I feel like I'm trapped in a box on a spreadsheet or confined to a bar in a graph or held, baffled and bouncing around, in the circles of a Venn diagram!

A mind dominated by this kind of thinking produces loads of mental pollution. When those thoughts become habitual and compulsive, we do, as in Lilly's analogy, become trapped. Our obsessiveness chokes life from us.

How are we supposed to find space, breathe deep, and be free?

In both Mason and Lilly, I hear something of myself (maybe you do too)—letting "what someone else might think" and anxious anticipation of the future distract me in the present moment. These mental habits can become so all-consuming that we find ourselves wishing our lives away, wasting our present moments. We think a real and better life will come "when I'm out of school" . . . "when our kids are grown" . . . "when we have grandkids" . . . "when I retire" . . . "when I get the promotion" . . . "once I can go on vacation."

At that point, life becomes a desperate crawl—inching toward a disappointing mirage. From the perspective of our present moment, the future is not yet real. It will be—but not now. The only peace-filled way to get to the future is to be thoughtfully engaged in the present moment. Then as we're present to our lives one moment at a time, the future will arrive. And having stayed in the present moment, we will be in that future in peace.

A Psalm 139 Self

Try this: instead of always nervously and restlessly waiting on the future, let the future wait on you. Don't let the future steal your peace by allowing it to be in charge of your heart, dictate your mind, or shape your soul. If we go through life simply reacting to what's going on in our busy minds and hectic world, we will forfeit the "Psalm 139 self" God intends us to be: ·

"You created my inmost being" becomes "I must create a self."
"You knit me together in my mother's womb" becomes "I feel fractured, like I'm falling apart."
"I praise you because I am fearfully and wonderfully made" becomes "I'd better hurry up and make something of myself."
"I was made in the secret place" becomes "I am no one unless I make it to such-and-such a place."
"Your eyes saw my unformed body" becomes "No one sees me or values me."
"All the days ordained for me were written in your book

before one of them came to be" becomes "I'd better cram a bunch of stuff in my calendar so I look busy, important, and worthy of respect."

When thoughts like these consume us, we live out of the screenplays we are writing in our minds, not out of those based in the will of God at our creation. We may get pretentious and start playacting. Our minds may become like the color commentators on televised sportscasts, and we begin to pick apart so much of our existence that very little room is left for confident living. The saddest thing is that in big swaths of our daily lives we get rewarded for such thinking. Our harsh judgments of ourselves suggest to others that we are serious and not thoughtless, dedicated to achieving perfection and not lazy or self-satisfied.

But that mindset has a treacherous shadow side: we lose our peace. We get isolated in our own heads. We are remote and stubborn rather than vulnerable and interactive. We are closed rather than open. We lose the ability to be a peaceful participant in the ups and downs of life.

Contentment

Scripture gives us a mental picture for the way to flee the anxious forecasting of the future and find peace in the present moment, not *reacting* in dread to a possible, predicted future but *responding* in peace to the present. This habit of the heart is grounded in the great life-shaping power of *contentment*.

Philippians 4:11–12: "I have learned to *be content* whatever
the circumstances . . . whether well fed or hungry,
whether living in plenty or in want" (emphasis mine).
Proverbs 15:16 (MSG): "*A simple life in the Fear-of-God*

is better than a rich life with a ton of headaches"
(emphasis mine).
1 Timothy 6:6: "Godliness with *contentment* is great gain"
(emphasis mine).
Hebrews 13:5: "Keep your lives free from the love of money
and *be content* with what you have" (emphasis mine).

If restless anxiety is a peace stealer, contentment is a powerful fertilizer for growing peace. Contentment is a peaceful ease of mind. It feels like deep, gratifying rest. Out of such a state, we can rise to meet the demands of life in peace and love. Discontentment, in contrast, sparks strife and anger; we grab what we want and harshly push away those who impede us.

An anxious and covetous mind leads us to believe wrong and harmful things, to engage in self-defeating, self-sabotaging self-talk. Self-doubts consume us: *Will I be able to get what I want?* Accusations against ourselves and others begin to fly. Doubts about God come to the forefront: *Will he come through for me? What if he doesn't—does that mean God does not exist or that he doesn't love me?*

We cannot reliably and consistently live a life of peace on the foundation of those doubts. Peace within is the overflow of being so loved by God that contentment is the natural state of our souls. From that place of provision, we are then free to love, forgive, and serve our neighbor.

Patience as You Grow

A big trick in the pursuit of peace is the intuitive notion that we must turn a great deal of attention on our interior selves. This is true, but as soon as we do, we confront the inner chaos I just described. Yet we must keep at it. We might do well to have a mature spiritual friend, counselor, or spiritual director help us.

As we push ahead, the damning voices will cease and "peace will indeed come, but it will be the fruit, not of pushing away distractions, but of meeting thoughts and feelings with stillness [in the present] instead of [judgmental] commentary."[1]

The pursuit of peace requires the cultivation of its close cousin—namely, patience. We can't beat ourselves up about our thoughts and feelings and simply use our wills to brush them away like so much sawdust on a shop floor. If we try that approach, we will find them to be more like spilled honey on the kitchen floor—requiring sustained attention and some elbow grease.

Rather than obsessing about our current state of growing in peace, instead of judging ourselves or wondering what others would think *if they only knew*, we are much better off simply noting the thoughts and feelings and moving on.[2]

The prime consideration for being at peace in the midst of our inner and outer realities is this: What occupies our mind—our thoughts and feelings? And *especially* this: What are our ideas and images of God? These ideas will prompt *feelings* or have feelings attached to them. Feelings are spontaneous and involuntary. They move us in one direction or another. For instance, hatred can imprison our mind, warp our soul, and lead us to use our human strength to harm another. Feelings of love, joy, and peace lead us in other directions—to work for the good of others.

What do you think occupied the mind of Jesus—the second person of the Holy Trinity? What were Jesus' ideas and images of God? Do you suppose they were accurate? Did they enable Jesus to be *functional*, as we use the term today? What was true for Jesus is true for us. That which we naturally, easily, and routinely *think* about God is what governs our actions—not the doctrines we've learned or the things we suppose we ought to believe. Paul encourages us that in the midst of whatever else we have going on, "you'll do best by filling your minds and meditating on things true, noble, reputable, authentic, compelling, gracious—the best, not the worst; the beautiful, not the ugly; things to praise, not things to curse" (Philippians 4:8 MSG).

Paul's encouragement can seem impractical, overly pious, or some kind of religious extra credit. But his words come in the most practical way in his letter to the Philippians. He is relating a few ways he would like to see the church at Philippi align more closely with the life of Christ within them. This is the mindset that makes Paul's words valid and valuable: *I am seeking to entrust my life to God such that the overflow of it is for the good of others.* When that is the overriding goal of one's life—at home, school, or work—we know that the pavers leading in that direction are imprinted with the words *true, honorable, just, pure, lovely, commendable, worthy of praise.* Each step livable.

Jesus is our model for this. He filled his mind with the relational love, wisdom, and power of the Holy Trinity. His mind was not filled, as ours often are, with bad thoughts and feelings about God. Thus he was not threatened by evil. He was able to leave his destiny in the hands of God. As a result, even in the midst of human pain, the ugliness of sin, the brutality of disease, and the harsh reality of demonization—and even in the face of death—he was freed to think of those realities through the lenses of beauty, goodness, and the supremacy of God.

Jesus' habit of thinking—he knew the love, wisdom, greatness, and goodness of God—and patterns of living—he was safe in the love and provision of God—are central to what he tried to teach the Twelve. They are at the core of what the Spirit seeks to impart to the church. After Jesus' death, a couple of his followers were walking out of Jerusalem back to their home. They were deeply confused. It seemed obvious that the crucifixion meant the end of everything Jesus believed and taught. On top of that, people seemed to be making up stories about a resurrection. You could say that these two dear people were filled with angst about all things religious, political, and social. And last but not least, they were confused by what seemed to them to be fake news that Jesus somehow was still alive. Their issues were very much like ours today.

And into their jumbled-up mixture of bewilderment, fear, and grief, "Jesus himself stood among them and said to them, 'Peace be with you'" (Luke 24:36). Peace? How? The betrayal by Judas was gut-wrenching. The soldiers were callous. The ruling powers were rude and dismissive. The death on the cross was excruciating. Jesus' friends appeared to be jumping ship. The stories coming from the vicinity of the tomb seemed truly unbelievable—too good to be true. So . . . really, Jesus, *peace*? Can human beings have peace in a whirlwind of that sort of agony? Yes, that is precisely the promise to those who are in Christ.

In the coming chapters, we'll put together what we've learned so far in order to explore what it means to be at peace with others—at peace for the sake of our relationships, for the sake of society.

Peace with God: Peace with God comes from sincerely seeking to embody his "Psalm 139" intentions for you. But do you often get caught in the trap of, and become controlled by, what others think of you? What can you do to lower the volume of critics and raise the volume of God's intention?

Peace Within: Peace within cannot be achieved without contentment. Are you content? If not, why not? What are you seeking that is worth the price of having a restless, discontent soul?

Peace for the Sake of the World: Those who are at peace for the sake of the world have a certain posture toward life—namely, a focus on that which is true, compelling, gracious, and the like (Philippians 4:8). People who live contrary to this are not pleasant to be around and thus lose their ability to have life-giving interactions with others. How do you assess yourself in this regard?

PEACE WITH OTHERS

CHAPTER 14

REJECTING FEAR-BASED HOSTILITY

Remind the people to . . . be ready to do whatever is good, to slander no one, to be peaceable and considerate, and always to be gentle toward everyone . . . [not like we used to live] in malice and envy, being hated and hating one another.

TITUS 3:1–3

No real dialogue is possible between somebody and a nobody.

HENRI NOUWEN, *REACHING OUT*

Teaching . . . asks for a mutual trust in which those who teach and those who want to learn can become present to each other, not as opponents, but as those who share the same struggle and search for the same truth.

HENRI NOUWEN, *REACHING OUT*

In 1875, you would have been hard-pressed to quickly find a book in a library. But in 1876, the Dewey Decimal System for classifying books was invented. One no longer had to stand, slowing turning this way and that, gazing through confused eyes at hundreds of shelves containing thousands of books, wondering where to start. The Dewey system celebrates the utilitarian goodness of the strict, clear categorizing of things: "A" is not "B"; "123" is not "456."

Thinking about libraries is a good way to gain an imagination for an important aspect of science called *taxonomy*. Taxonomy dictates how various things should be named, described, and classified. Categories, classes, and types are crucial to all scientific fields. Think of cancer cells versus healthy cells. Arranging and ordering things are completely normal human activities.

Difference, and the knowledge of it, is good. Without the ability to recognize and name dissimilarities, human life would not function well. Strict uniformity and the denial of distinction are not useful views of the world. But with the wrong heart motivations, calling out differences is destructive.

For instance, polarities increasingly mark our intellectual frameworks and emotional landscapes. These polarizations create schisms, divisions, and splits of all kinds, from the deeply personal to the broadly institutional. With the zeal of a taxonomist in a bad mood, we harshly name and categorize people, ideas, and events. We then use "otherness" as the (often subconscious) rationale for dehumanizing words and actions. The ability to see differences can become a weapon.

We need a new framework for all this naming to keep it from so often turning to judging and dismissing. The modern rhetoric in partisan politics and on current social media is not helping us. It is driving us further apart. And we are losing a healthy sense of self. As a songwriter put it, "If I feel as though my sole identity is as a walking representative of my church, my denomination, or my political party, then my speech and creativity are reduced to propaganda."[1]

We need a path that helps us *name* without *name-calling*. But to avoid name-calling, we cannot simply assert that "everything is the same." We don't want our naming of things to lead to disengagement with people or modern culture, to the point where we say, "Those guys are bad and not worthy of my attention!" This is not a call to ignore evil, suffering, or injustice. It is possible for a cardiologist to name reality ("Your blood pressure has gotten a bit high") without name-calling ("You're such a stupid idiot; I told you to watch your salt intake!"). Judgmental name-calling commonly comes from anxious, controlling impulses. Giving in to those impulses cannot make for any kind of peace—with God, within, or in the world.

From Xenophobia to Xenophilia

When I was in junior high school, my brother, Dennis, was killed in Vietnam. In the previous years, television and radio reports of the Vietnam war had taught us to demonize and dehumanize the Viet Cong to such a degree that we could rationalize killing more than one million of them, many of whom were women and children. So when Dennis was hit by a mortar shell, it felt natural that my heart was consumed with hatred. I regularly dreamed of revenge. You can imagine my surprise when, a decade later, a young couple in our church came to me and asked if the church would help fund the adoption of Vietnamese children. I take no credit for it, but I was shocked at the easy yes that sprang up in my heart. I genuinely wanted to help. The purpose of this chapter and the next is to inspire transitions from xenophobia (fear of those unlike us) to xenophilia (love of those unlike us).[2]

Fear of *the other*—other people, other perspectives, other outcomes—marks our day. We see xenophobia illustrated in the arenas of partisan politics, racism, immigration, and sexuality. Happily, the possibility of the spiritual formation of the human soul is open before us, such that xenophobia is replaced with confident, grounded, peaceful xenophilia. Our model here is Trinitarian: making space for and richly interacting with *the Other(s)* is not foreign to God—it is the very definition of who he is.

The Greek term *xenophobia* is literally translated "stranger fearing." We typically think of it as having an aversion to people or cultures that are unfamiliar or an instinctual dislike of those who are not like us. Xenophobia often includes a fear of the unknown—*the other* who is unknown to us. Dislike and fear lead to prejudging. Xenophobia includes the tendency to see personal qualities of difference and then to fear or hate the variation: ethnicity, age, gender, sexuality, political affiliation. Based on these quick, surface observations of externals, we think we know the character of the person in front of us. People or things that are not normal, standard, or common seem strange to us and make us feel uncomfortable. Based on our judgment of who is odd and therefore undesirable, we think we can justify various forms of harm or exclusion.

Let's probe our instincts a bit. Which is peculiar—chopsticks or forks? Western musical scales or Eastern? Who is it that has an accent—the American Southerner or someone from China? Xenophobia is a result of the overflow of believing that one's own self and way of life are natural and correct. This way of thinking can stem from a sense of superiority. It's almost always true that such judgments are based on some level of incomplete knowledge or preconceptions of another person or culture. These judgments lead to conflicts between people and nations.

The desire to belong to a group is a deeply human experience. Xenophobia is instinctually thought to be a way to facilitate the belonging of similar people. But the need to belong does not need to be enforced by suspicion and cynicism toward others. Being in one group does not mean we have to see others as threats. Being in a certain group does not give us permission to see others in demeaning ways. Disparaging another subset of people does not make our group better. Rather, it makes us into worse sorts of human beings. Yet this behavior clearly kills peace and fuels strife and conflict in families, churches, denominations, and political parties.

Why do we assume that differentness requires conflict? When we engage in xenophobic attitudes and behaviors, we make life harder for others—which is the polar opposite of our call to love and serve in gentle peace. Loving and serving others brings peace to our soul and also brings peace and well-being to the lives of others. Harboring fear of the other, in contrast, pollutes our soul with harsh judgmentalism and leads to harming others.

We are called to take the alternate route paved with the patient love of seeing others as people created in God's image. This road is not strewn with the sins of pride, judgmentalism, and vanity—qualities we assume we need if we are to keep our group pure and superior, which leads to the belief that we have the right to judge others.

Who Is *the Other?*

My aim here is for us to be able to experience difference in an instinctually positive way, only coming to think otherwise upon commonsense evidence. In xenophilia, we don't judge a person's worth or capabilities based on first glance. Rather, we cultivate the habits of heart that lead us to wonder, *Who is this person? What do they care about, laugh about, cry about? What are their gifts, talents, and potential?* In short, in coming to have a predisposition of loving the other, we consider people through the lens of Psalm 8:3–5:

When I consider your heavens,
　　the work of your fingers,
the moon and the stars,
　　which you have set in place,
what is mankind that you are mindful of them,
　　human beings that you care for them?

You have made them a little lower than the angels
　　and crowned them with glory and honor.

Picture someone around whom you feel the uncomfortable feeling of otherness, self-consciousness, or self-righteous fear. Now picture this person through the lens of Psalm 8. Relate them first to God. Then relate them to yourself via neighbor love. If you struggle to do those things, you are not alone. You may struggle, but it is a necessary work. The help is in the psalm: we are all creatures made in the image of God, crowned with glory and honor.

Coming to love the people we have contact with is possible. It is the will of God. We just need to work at it a bit by cultivating new habits of the heart.

Xenophilia within Diversity

There is no such thing as a noncontextual life. Every person is situated in a time and space and has a worldview. We live in a stressful, transitional, global, technological moment when everything feels up for grabs—and is being grabbed for by means of conflict. Swift changes in culture cause siege mentalities rooted in desperate fear. And when it comes to ideas for cultural engagement, fear is a very bad master. In our era, it has become normal to think that peace will come through war. For religious people this has meant *culture wars*. But gaining political power and winning culture wars are not biblical categories.

Does the desire to reclaim, transform, redeem, resist, or defy something justify ceaseless conflict? Are other paths available to us—such as the humble, cruciform one walked by Jesus? Can you imagine a major leader in business, education, military, or politics saying, as Jesus did, "Follow me; do it my way. I am gentle and humble in heart." Eugene Peterson wrote, "When it comes to doing something about what is wrong in the world, Jesus is best known for his fondness for the insignificant, the invisible, the quiet, the slow–yeast, salt, seeds, light. And manure."[3]

Take, for instance, the 1990s version of the culture wars: the weapons that were used by the right to defeat the left are now used among warring factions of the right as they battle over who, on any given issue, is far enough to the right on the political or religious spectrum. And the same practices are used as the left wars within itself. Where one is on a religious or political spectrum is not ultimately definitive. The modern political scales on which we weigh ourselves are inventions of humankind. They are artificial constructs. In sharp contrast, the soul of a human being, while unseen, is concretely real. The heart/soul each one of us possesses is what makes us who we are. I refuse the definitions of political manipulators. I accept, welcome, and give myself to the label "follower of Jesus," resolving to seek truth wherever it exists and learning to live in the kingdom of God as a person of gentle peace, the overflow of which comes to expression in loving neighbor and enemy.

A xenophobia-fueled state of *war* too often exists in personal and civic relationships. Current techniques of contemporary war include firing off destructive tweets, writing incendiary posts, thinking the worst of others and the best of ourselves, shouting others down, and passing on rumors that destroy reputations. We think, *Well, we* must *respond in this way. The issues are important, and* they *are the enemy. What else do you do with enemies other than use overwhelming force to break them down in defeat?*

What do you think it would mean to take Jesus' words about loving one's enemy seriously? Let's do a bit of honest reflection: Do we find ourselves daydreaming about ways to humiliate someone online or about becoming persons of gentle peace, those who exude grace and generosity to others, thus enhancing their lives? Whichever internal reality is true of us, it is the trellis on which the flowers of our relational life grow.

Will We Enjoy Heaven?

One of the first things we're likely to notice about heaven is the vast diversity of human souls. Vast diversity will be obvious in heaven. Do you imagine you will celebrate that reality, or will you find it off-putting?

What if in heaven those who created humanity's first tools in the Stone Age are really upset and frightened by Roombas? What if those who came to age within recorded history say to those who lived in pre-history, "We do not acknowledge your humanity!" What if people are offended by being told that they lived in the Dark Ages? What if modern environmentalists want to form gangs to beat up the inventors who fomented the Industrial Revolution? Will Luddites form battle plans to reduce the Silicon Valley to rubble?

Perhaps nothing like what I suggest will be possible in heaven. Maybe we can rely on the promises of our full transformation to loving others suggested in such Scriptures as 1 Corinthians 15:51–52 ("We will not all sleep, but we will all be changed—in a flash, in the twinkling of an eye"); Matthew 13:43 ("Then the righteous will shine like the sun"); Luke 20:36 ("They are like the angels"); and Romans 8:17 ("We are . . . co-heirs with Christ . . . that we may also share in his glory").

If these Scriptures teach that the perfections of heaven will not allow temptations to xenophobia, division, and dehumanization, then wouldn't you like to live now as a person of loving peace in alignment with this extraordinary vision? I'm not asking if you think you *can* do it perfectly in this life; I'm asking if you *want* to. We will not come anywhere near being peace-filled, peacemaking "lovers of the other" until it is a sincere desire of our hearts and determination of our wills. God does not bully us into taking on his heart. He invites us to follow Jesus, to ever increasingly adopt his sacred heart—a heart in which willing the harm of others has no space, no possibility, no potential. Our calling is to give ourselves to Jesus as his students in kingdom living such that we increasingly, by grace and with joy, conduct ourselves now as we will conduct ourselves then.

Fear of the other does not have to rule us. We can completely flip our hearts to an instinctual love of difference. Come with me to the next pages, and I'll explain what I mean.

Peace with God: It is not possible to dismiss, despise, or hate others and be at peace with God. Compile a list of your least favorite people. Then work with God to find a way to move in the direction of loving them and seeking their good.

Peace Within: Do you have anxiety that is rooted in the fear of others? Distress when it comes to differences? In heaven, all of this inner noise will be gone. Imagine being in that fearless state, and welcome the peace it brings. Begin to act *now* as you will act *then*. Over time, you will be transformed.

Peace for the Sake of the World: Labeling others and being in constant tension with them make us less than winsome people to be around. Our ability to be at peace for the sake of the world is harmed. How could your relational posture change if you were empowered to see everyone through the eyes of Psalm 8, realizing that people are the masterpiece of God's creation—just a bit lower than the angels—and crowned with glory and honor?

CHAPTER 15

LOVING THE OTHER

*Keep on loving one another as brothers and
sisters. Do not forget to show hospitality to
strangers.*

HEBREWS 13:1–2

*After this I looked, and there before me was
a great multitude that no one could count,
from every nation, tribe, people and language,
standing before the throne and before the
Lamb.*

REVELATION 7:9

M om, why is that lady Black?" My wife fainted. Just kidding—
but she wanted a hole to appear in the floor through which
she could disappear! Our son, upon seeing a Black person for the
first time, barely able to talk, exclaimed those words loud enough
for the whole "cookies and crackers" aisle to hear. Thank God
for the grace and good humor of our Black neighbor—and in
hindsight I apologize that she had to experience that moment.

Noticing "the other" is a built-in feature of humanity. It is not an entirely bad thing. Harm comes when seeing difference shifts to judging other people to be wrong, bad, scary, or untrustworthy. Love of the other is not automatic. Most people have to go through a process of maturity to instinctually love people of other cultures and ethnicities. Our interior lives sometimes block it. In this chapter, we'll explore some common hindrances and strong bridges to xenophilia—the natural love of those who are different from us.

Judge Not

Fear-based divisions are all around us. They are becoming more frequent and more intense. Discord and disunion are the result of the sin of xenophobia. Without intending to blame any one source, but just to cite an example of the forces of division among us. The *Wall Street Journal* filed a chilling report that Facebook's own research in 2018 revealed that "our algorithms exploit the human brain's attraction to divisiveness . . . If left unchecked, Facebook would feed users 'more and more divisive content in an effort to gain user attention and increase time on the platform.'"[1] An article in the *Washington Post* asserted that "we're living, in effect, in a big anger incubator."[2] A Pew research study reveals that "just 12% of Americans say they are satisfied with the way things are going in this country today . . . About seven-in-ten Americans (71%) say they feel angry about the state of the country these days, while roughly two-thirds (66%) say they feel fearful."[3]

When we feel pressed for any given reason or feel our response can be justified by "how much I care" or "how passionate I am" about an issue, *condemnation of others* becomes a go-to response. But Jesus taught that we must not judge one another; rather, we are to treat others in the noncondemning way we want to be treated:

"Do not judge, or you too will be judged. For in the same way you judge others, you will be judged . . .

"Why do you look at the speck of sawdust in your brother's eye and pay no attention to the plank in your own eye? How can you say to your brother, 'Let me take the speck out of your eye,' when all the time there is a plank in your own eye? You hypocrite, first take the plank out of your own eye, and then you will see clearly to remove the speck from your brother's eye . . .

"So in everything, do to others what you would have them do to you, for this sums up the Law and the Prophets."

MATTHEW 7:1–5, 12

Jesus is not saying, "Have no thoughts," or "Lose the human ability to make things distinct," or "Give up knowing right from wrong," or "Hide your eyes from injustice." He is teaching that our views of others must be tempered by the knowledge of our imperfect observations about them. We have a plank in our eye. And if we are wrong about something, have a blind spot, or are somehow deceived, we need to be helped to see the truth of things with an attitude of respect and love.

The belief that everyone is created in the image of God shapes my fundamental imagination for how to treat others in peace. A biblical or theological anthropology relates human beings first to God and then to all that God created—especially those created in God's image.[4] This embraces our entire social circle—including enemies. A biblical anthropology sees all people of every kind as primarily defined by the virtue of being created in the image of God with the purpose of being his creative, cooperative friends.

By God's initiative, every person has a destiny to which they are summoned. Each human being is invited into the mission and purposes of God. Within God's intention for humanity, we are all one in a doubly powerful way: we are created as one blood, and we are re-created by the blood of Jesus and sent into the world in peace as one people. Paul's dream for this has always gotten my attention, even if it may seem to be unattainable at this moment in history.

> There is neither Jew nor Gentile, neither slave nor free, nor is there male and female, for you are all one in Christ Jesus.
>
> GALATIANS 3:28

> [In Christ] there is no Gentile or Jew,. circumcised or uncircumcised, barbarian, Scythian, slave or free, but Christ is all, and is in all.
>
> COLOSSIANS 3:11

But with regard to Paul's vision, sin has distorted and broken our will for inclusion and our quest for unity in multifaceted ways. We then distort and mistreat others. The cycle goes on and on—helped along by powerful technological devices. But the problem doesn't lie in social media platforms. If he were walking the earth today, Jesus might say, "Out of the overflow of the heart the thumbs doth tweet." We are trapped in the brokenness of the fall until we give ourselves to Jesus as his apprentices in kingdom living who are learning to love God and his ways, our neighbors, and our enemies.

In opposition to knee-jerk condemnation rooted in judgment, we need to cultivate, model, and teach the practical goodness of restraint; of humble tentativeness, of listening, of seeking first to understand and only then to be understood. This doesn't mean we don't have clarity about injustice, morality and ethics, or social policy. It just means that I'd like you to show me a time when Jesus justified "going off on someone" in the sinful ways that are so routine today.[5] And Jesus saw reality without a

plank in his eye. He accurately saw the truth of the full pano-
rama of human sin and error. Yet this insight did not lead him
to rationalize hateful words; rather, his love and grace compelled
attitudes and actions of peace and patience.

Certain things in human life lead to the degradation of people
(such as racism), and this needs to change *now*. But as we work for
change, we must consider this truth: incalculable harm has been
done to human beings in the name of doing good; all we need
to do is recall the various "isms" of the twentieth century that
led to world wars. We don't see in Scripture merely *what needs
fixing*; we see God's idea for *how to fix it*. His plan is "cruciform"
in presence and "resurrection" in hope. We work against injustice
best when we work out of transformed inner lives.

Vanity

Vanity is a common source of judgmentalism and xenophobia.
Vanity assumes a sense of inflated pride or an exaggerated opinion
of oneself or one's talents, looks, or wealth. Vanity shapes a way
of living that is empty and unfulfilling, lacking satisfying sub-
stance. It portrays a life that is hollow, deficient in reality. Vanity
is marked by futile desires and immature attempts at success and
meaningless pleasure. It implies a certain kind of rootlessness in
pursuit of fleeting experiences and short-lived achievements. It
leads to despair. The vision of the New Testament includes the
healing of this common human anguish.

Jesus promised to give water that truly quenches thirst
(John 4:13–14) and food that satisfies and nourishes (John 6:51).
Putting one's confidence in Jesus' invitation and pursuing its
reality is a strong antidote to vanity and the toxic sin that flows
from it.

Jesus, knowing the vain and transitory nature of our short life
on earth, gave us the mental model for finding stable peace—and

thereby stripping away our xenophobia in our quest to become persons of peace. He said, "Don't vainly worry about your life. Your heavenly Father knows what you really need, so seek first God's kingdom and God's righteousness, and then you can be at humble peace, knowing that everything else you need will be given to you as well" (Matthew 6:25–33, my paraphrase).

Modesty

If vanity is the snakebite of a proud, self-focused expression of self, the cultivation of modesty is the antivenom. Those who exhibit modesty are unassuming and restrained in their estimation of their abilities. Modest people feel no need to parade who they are, like a peacock in full display, in order to make themselves look superior to others. Modest people are unpretentious and have a healthy sense of self. They have no need for fanfare and thus have no desire to pretend they have more or are more than others.

You can imagine how modesty results from inner peace, facilitates peace with others, and therefore is a cure for xenophobia. Modest people are too busy listening and learning to experience reflexive fear or judgment when it comes to differences. Rather than needing others to hear their brilliant thoughts, they are driven by a loving and welcoming curiosity. Modesty—along with its close relative, humility—is a conduit for godliness that breaks the cycle of fear and rejection.

Love One Another

One of the Bible's simplest imperatives contains only three words: *love one another.* Yet love seems to be missing in most cultural, social, and personal squabbles. Where there is genuine love, there is hope for a better future marked by discovery, hope for having one's perspective sharpened and improved. Without love, we have only the squabbling status quo—or regression into ever-deepening cycles of dismissiveness, abuse, rejection, and violence.

Envisioned in Jesus' call to "love one another" (John 13:34) are the attributes of xenophilia—the commitment to will the good of others. Jesus' apostles share their insights about embodying the whole spectrum of love in the routine activities of our lives (my paraphrases):

- No one can engage in xenophobia when they are completely humble and gentle, patient, bearing with one another in love, and kind and compassionate to one another, forgiving each other, just as in Christ God forgave them (Ephesians 4:2, 32).
- Seekers of peace and lovers of the other must be devoted to one another in love and honor one another above themselves (Romans 12:10).
- Those who seek peace with others rather than judge them live in harmony with one another. They are not proud but are willing to associate with people of low position. They are not conceited (Romans 12:16). They accept one another, just as Christ accepted them (15:7).
- Those living in peace and love make sure they do not pay back wrong for wrong but are always striving to do what is good for each other and everyone else (1 Thessalonians 5:15).
- In pursuit of humble, gentle modesty, those who embrace xenophilia do nothing out of selfish ambition or vain conceit; rather, in humility they value others above themselves (Philippians 2:3).
- Peace seekers consistently consider how they can spur one another on toward love and good deeds (Hebrews 10:24).

This is the New Testament vision for interaction with others, including with those who are different from us. It is stunning. Its potential for human good is unsurpassed. It is a certain kind of life—the life of Jesus welcomed into our lives so that, by means of the power of the Holy Spirit, love of other people, cultures, and customs is genuine and natural, having displaced our former fear and disdain of others.

For me, thinking about the culture and customs of the Holy Trinity is a good, imaginative way to think about *otherness*. God exists as a trinity of beings. No being of the Trinity is afraid of the distinctness of the other—Father, Son, and Holy Spirit. Nor are they scared to interact with the utter otherness of human beings. Rather, the Father so loved humanity that the Son and the Spirit came to earth to save, empower, and deploy a people marked by God himself.

This people—the church, the people of God—is meant to live in similar otherness: loving each other, not fearing or hating the other. If this vision were to be implemented, church boards would be healed of nasty divisions. We would make the best of the sad creation of denominations as the love of the Trinity spills over into our interactions and doctrinal conversations. Imagine courteous, considerate connections in church councils. Imagine denominations valuing differences, showing empathy for the stories and histories of others, appreciating each other from the heart.

Knowing no human person or culture is perfect should bring a natural and necessary humility that yields a welcoming, "assume the best until proven wrong" love of the other. Holding negative views of people until they prove they've met the standards we've set for them is not an example of clarity or strength; it is an example of arrogance and fear, which almost always manifest themselves in destructive behaviors. To the contrary, seeking to love each other as modeled by the Trinity gives us the best possible footing to be the church at peace for the world.

This Is Our Father's World

Whatever anxiety-producing things are happening around the world or in our neighborhoods, here is what we can know with absolute certainty: this is *our Father's* world. The Trinity—Father, Son, and Spirit—is the world's (and our) Creator, Savior, and Sustaining Superintendent. And humanity remains God's project. We live in a Trinitarian-bathed world that, by God's loving, wise design, is perfectly suited to finding him and serving others in gentle, peaceful love. The divine intention for creation is not (and never will be) in doubt—even if our newsfeeds scream otherwise. We can be totally assured of the comprehensive completion of God's intention in creation. One day, Jesus will hand over the kingdom to his Father, and everything will be perfect. No more tears or pain—just the knowledge that God is God and that he has been right all along. He has been working on our behalf from creation right up to the inbreaking of a new heaven and a new earth. Modeling our lives on the incarnate Christ who fills creation, we are invited to participate now in his life—a life marked by peace, humility, and self-sacrificial love.

We are always safe and thus at peace when we derive our lives from and live them within the kingdom of God as apprentices of Jesus. Having cultivated deep inner peace, we never again need to use illicit means to deal with our anxiety. We can let go of our habits of sinning in order to protect ourselves, provide for ourselves, or secure ourselves from *the other.* This means the church, the people of God, can cultivate habits of the heart out of which we love extravagantly, take risks joyfully, and forgive generously. Given the omnipotence of the God we serve, favor, money, and power are not zero-sum issues. Thus we never need to fight, quarrel, or grab. We are at peace.

No Need to Fear

We've said that xenophobia is commonly produced by, or at least accompanied by, fear. In the midst of diversity, we sense our otherness and can feel alone. This daunting feeling fuels fight or flight, attack or withdrawal. Both are deeply painful to their recipients. In xenophilia, we are given a third way—namely, to simply join with God, who is already present and at work in his world. We sometimes feel disoriented by differences. In those instances, ask yourself, *What do I think God is feeling in this moment?* It is consistent with the creation narratives to believe that he rejoices at his diverse creativity. This reality invites us to move toward this peaceful inner posture: *I am not alone in my ethnicity, body shape, skin tone, or thoughts and feelings. I am not abandoned in a huge crowd of differences. God is there. His presence is grace.*

For those who notice it, receive it, and interact with it, this grace becomes a settling, grounding, and enlivening peace. It means we never have to justify anti-peace behaviors that we adopt because we're "trying to make something important happen." When we let go of our disordered desires, we give ourselves over to becoming the cooperative friends of God, who is actively present in our everyday lives. When our hearts know that God is shepherding his creation to its intended completion, we are at peace. We can live in love and peace with others who also live under God's powerful care.

Toward Xenophilia

God has revealed himself as *God of the other.* A powerful passage from Deuteronomy declares: "For the LORD your God is God of gods and Lord of lords, the great God, mighty and awesome, who shows no partiality and accepts no bribes. He defends the cause of the fatherless and the widow, and loves the foreigner residing among you, giving them food and clothing. And you are to love those who are foreigners, for you yourselves were foreigners in Egypt" (Deuteronomy 10:17–19). Psalm 101:5 reads, "Whoever slanders their neighbor in secret, I will put to silence; whoever has haughty eyes and a proud heart, I will not tolerate."

Passages like these are revealing and moving. But if we're honest, most of us have to admit that *loving the other* does not come naturally. It's also true that many of us sincerely do want to overcome our prejudices. Here are several ideas for heading in that direction:

- *Embrace Jesus' gospel of the kingdom.* When pressed by others, Jesus always explained his controversial love of the other on the basis of the inbreaking of his Father's reign and his obedience to it. If we want the fruit of positive, fearless love that approximates the way of Jesus, we must learn to live, teach, and minister in his footsteps.

- *Don't fear culture.* Culture bashing, culture hating, and culture warring can never be the seedbed of loving the other, and thus they are not conducive to peace. We will be too busy being suspicious and controlled by our prejudices and cynicism. Rather, in gentle peace we want to pivot toward a natural and easy love of God's creation—even the bits that make us anxious.

- *Rely on the Holy Spirit.* Within the one-blood but vastly diverse humanity, the beautiful creativity of the Holy Spirit generates and oversees the diversity of gifts, talents, skills, and callings in the church. In short, much of what we see as scary differences can be trusted as the work of the Spirit. It is the Holy Spirit who guides, inspires, authorizes, empowers, and engifts Christian life and ministry such that we come to joyfully love all that God loves—his whole, varied creation.

- *Pursue spiritual transformation.* The spiritual formation of our hearts must underlie and animate the pursuit of xenophilia. Through becoming Jesus' lifelong students in kingdom living, we become the kind of people who *can* and *will* routinely love the other. As we are formed into the likeness of Christ, we share more and more in God's affection and love for others. We grow in kindheartedness toward the other. We empathize with, pray for, and work in behalf of others in a heart-renovated, self-sacrificing manner. Freed from the drudgery of fear, we come to love others in a joy-filled way. As we gently work our way to stillness of soul, tranquility of heart, lightness of disposition, and peace of mind, we become human as God intended—lovers who will the good of the diverse persons we interact with.

When we have moved away from xenophobia and toward xenophilia, we are poised to pursue peace with others, which is our topic in the next chapter.

Peace with God: We can only have peace with God when we respect and love the pinnacle of his creation—human beings. Is this love natural or unnatural for you? Why? Take some time to see a difficult person through the lens of a theological anthropology. Relate them first to God as his creation, and notice what that does to your heart, mind, and will.

Peace Within: "This is my Father's world; I rest me in the thought." Sit quietly for a few moments with that lyric;

rest in the thought that nothing that is happening in the world steals it away from God and his will for it. As you rest, what effect on your soul do you notice?

Peace for the Sake of the World: This chapter moved us away from judging and toward loving one another and being at peace with others. Can you see how these practices change your posture in the world, your countenance, and your tone of voice? Imagine how these changes enable you to become an agent of peace in the world.

CHAPTER 16

PURSUING PEACE WITH OTHERS

*If it is possible, as far as it depends on you, live
at peace with everyone.*

ROMANS 12:18

Sitting around the committee table, we were all startled but
not really shocked to hear a symphony of agitated voices ris-
ing: "But he is so wrong!" "I can't help it—she is an idiot!" "I
don't trust him!" "She is just out to get whatever she can; she
doesn't care about us!" "He's a liar!" "She is just plain evil." So go
far too many conversations around various other tables as well.
Discussions about national politics (and state and local too) are
sure to elicit such remarks. Staff meetings at work can devolve
into shaming, engaging in ad hominem attacks, and questioning
people's motives. Even Little League committee meetings can get
mired in the mud of such language. Comments like these are not
unheard of at HOA board meetings. Nor is it rare, sadly enough,
that church members wound others with such comments in
church council meetings.

The Gospels and the letters of the New Testament have a

different vision for human interaction. They command over and over: "Be at peace with each other" (Mark 9:50); "Live in peace with each other" (1 Thessalonians 5:13).

Paul had the outlandish idea that we should be at peace with our leaders and with each other. I wonder what Paul might have said if he was writing in the age of Twitter. Peace doesn't seem feasible in our age of rage. After thousands of years of Jewish prophecy and Christian ethical thought, why is peace so elusive? What explains the giant gap between biblical teaching and human behavior?

I've thought about this a great deal. I wonder if we are where we are because *peace is not our first priority*. At least not consistently. Maybe we want peace when we want it, when conflict is not in our best interest. But when conflict *is* in our interest, we confront a stark reality: we want something else more than we want goodwill. Peace gets sidelined in favor of what we really want.

The Things That Would Bring You Peace

Jesus had a firsthand view of this tension as it played out among his contemporaries. Luke 19:41–42 reads, "As he approached Jerusalem and saw the city, he wept over it and said, 'If you, even you, had only known on this day what would bring you peace— but now it is hidden from your eyes.'"

In the Jerusalem of Jesus' era, conflict flourished. The Holy City was the stage on which many false messiahs sought to act. They were more like politicians or warlords. They ginned up anger and hatred toward Rome. They stirred war-producing loathing among various Jewish factions. They hoped their leadership would lead to open rebellion.

Jesus knew these things would not bring lasting peace, but rather cycles of revenge and conflict. Warhorses, chariots, armies, and political alliances did not mark Jesus' imagination and commitments. Rather, his approach fulfilled the biblical imagery of Zechariah 9:9–10. On his way to the cross, Jesus came powerfully into Jerusalem on a humble colt of a donkey. His entrance to the place from which true peace would begin and move toward its full flowering in the new heaven and the new earth was marked by humble peace, not by an anxious striving for the ancient version of clicks, eyeballs, and social media influence. Jesus' gentle goodwill launched a kingdom movement that radiated love, righteousness, joy, and peace.

Jesus taught that in the kingdom of God "blessed are the peacemakers" (Matthew 5:9). *Blessed* can be translated as "well-off" or "happy." This fortunate life, which is to be congratulated, comes precisely from receiving and extending God's peace. An inner life of conflict that manifests itself in constant battles with others makes for a life that is "poor-off" and "unhappy." This life is not to be celebrated but pitied. We intuitively know this about the life of strained relationships, yet we seem unable to get out of its grip. Why? We are readily willing and able to conjure up powerful justifications for anxiety and conflict. Our disordered desires overwhelm any longing for peace. We may theoretically think of peace as a good, true, or right idea, but such thinking does not usually result in consistent peace. Why? Because we love something more.

To get into Jesus' mind when it comes to the things that bring peace, let's recall a few of his teachings.

The Golden Rule

Jesus said, "Do to others whatever you would like them to do to you. This is the essence of all that is taught in the law and the prophets" (Matthew 7:12 NLT).

The Golden Rule is meant to lead Christ followers to be devoted to the good, the justice, the flourishing of the people around us. It conveys a significant ethical dimension of spiritual formation. It is a guide in searching for an ethical interior from which good, right, and worthwhile words and actions come. Other religions and systems of ethics have something called the "Silver Rule": "Don't do to others want you don't want done to you."[1]

Jesus' kingdom reality reaches far beyond the mere absence of doing harm to others. Jesus is calling for positive love of others—which, of course, rules out injuring others and instead entails alleviating their suffering. Jesus invites us to follow him to become the kind of people who aim to add significant prosperity, of whatever kind is needed, to the lives of others.

If everyone were to do this, we would all live in peace. But comparatively few people rearrange their lives to fit the powerful truth of this simple vision. Just think of the ways people proudly brag about their anti-peace rhetoric:

- Boy, did I get in her face!
- I didn't take any $&*# from him!
- He tried to give it to me, but I gave it back worse—that'll teach him!

A few basic practices need to be put in place so that we might become the persons Jesus envisions. First, we must learn to be *considerate*. This means we *consider* others, noticing their existence, not just our own. We imagine ourselves in the place of the one receiving our attitudes, words, or actions. We become attentive to their needs. We become good listeners. We develop a certain intuition about the state of others and practice empathy for anything and everything we come to know about them. We respect others and care for them. Patience, thoughtfulness, selflessness, and sympathy become intermediate goals that serve our long-term spiritual objective, namely, Christlikeness for the sake of others.

Wow, you may be thinking to yourself, *that sounds like a difficult transformation!* Yes, most likely. But let's set aside the struggle for a moment to ask, *What do I desire? Do I want to become a considerate person? Am I willing to arrange the activities of my life to do so?* We can't pursue the peace that comes from the Golden Rule unless our answers are yes.

Second, the Golden Rule requires taking *initiative.* The command is not to refrain from maltreatment but to actively *do* for others the good you'd like them to do for you. *Initiative* means we see what needs to be done—out of the consideration we have developed—and we do it without prompting from others. Like your roommate actually doing the dishes for once or a child taking out the trash or walking the dog or doing homework without being asked. It's a willingness to take responsibility, to take action. We want to become resourceful, determined, and resilient in our promotion of the good. *The Message* illumines Jesus' words: "Here is a simple, rule-of-thumb guide for behavior: Ask yourself what you want people to do for you, then grab the initiative and do it for *them.* Add up God's Law and Prophets and this is what you get" (Matthew 7:12, italics in original).

This is tough when one's highest priority is self. Which means, thirdly, we need to make our way to *selflessness* and then on to *altruism.* In a healthy, non-codependent way, we prioritize the needs of others so we are a benefit to them even if it costs us or we never get any credit for it. Altruistic selflessness implies being kind, gracious, and generous. It comes to expression in doing good to others without expecting anything in return.

Fulfilling the Law and the Prophets

The second sentence of the Golden Rule is crucial too: "This is the essence of all that is taught in the law and the prophets" (Matthew 7:12 NLT). When held together, the two sentences keep

Jesus' words from becoming a mere religious or idealistic cliché. The second sentence gives context, grounding, orientation, and an end goal to positive, loving actions toward others.

"The law and the prophets" refers to the whole revelation of divine will in the long story of God and his people. It is the framework on which biblical ethics is built. Jesus is summing up, in a representative way, all the commands and teachings of Israel to "do to others whatever you would like them to do to you."

Jesus says something similar in a scene in which the religious leaders were trying to trip him up. One of them asked him, "Teacher, which is the greatest commandment in the Law?" Jesus replied: "'Love the Lord your God with all your heart and with all your soul and with all your mind.' This is the first and greatest commandment. And the second is like it: 'Love your neighbor as yourself.' All the Law and the Prophets hang on these two commandments" (Matthew 22:35–40). Think of these two commandments—*love God, love your neighbor*—as the two hands of Jesus shaping us as if we were pliable clay on a potter's wheel.

"God, let me be shaped according to your will" is a constant and important prayer of mine. From the point of view of lived experience, this prayer creates the rich soil in which peace can grow. It means I've stopped fighting myself, have thrown off the yoke of others' expectations, and have embraced God's divine will. Almost every day, I pray something like, "Holy Spirit, untwist the twisted parts of me. I yield to your power to rebend me and make me straight, in plumb line with your will for me. I open myself to the reign of God's kingdom, to the guidance of the Spirit, to the provision of the Great Shepherd—"I will fear no evil, for you are with me; your rod and your staff, they comfort me" (Psalm 23:4).

When I was a young convert in the Jesus Movement of the mid-1970s, we'd often sing a chorus that planted seeds of good desire and by its repetitive singing worked its ideas deep into my heart: "Spirit of the living God, fall afresh on me. Melt me, mold me, fill me, use me."[2]

In all the forty-five years I have been walking with the Lord, I don't think there has been a deeper heart cry or more honest sung prayer than this: *Melt me . . . mold me . . . fill me . . . use me.* I still remember the goose bumps, the lump in my throat—and sometimes big tears as I repeatedly committed and recommitted my life to God. Such surrender is indispensable to finding peace with God, peace within, and peace with others.

I don't pretend to be some sort of a spiritual hero. I don't think I even realized the importance of my heart cry facilitated by that song. But as I look back, I believe it dug up the soil of my heart and soul, readying it for spiritual seeds to be planted in me. I now know the intuitive surrender implied in the song is part of what will bring us peace.

In the next few chapters, we'll look at specific practices for welcoming peace and discuss how peace assists us in times of trial and temptation.

Peace with God: We cannot have peace with God if we're cultivating conflict with others. With whom do you need to drop a conflict? What is the first step in doing so? Make a plan to take that first step, and be encouraged to know that increased peace with God awaits.

Peace Within: Is there something in you that repeatedly wants to "get in people's faces"? This attitude does not flow out of a peace within; it flows out of a hostility within. Ask the Holy Spirit to help you discern what steps you can take to diminish hostility and to foster patient love.

Peace for the Sake of the World: The world needs people who seek to be ambassadors of the things that bring peace. What is your vision for becoming such a person? Is there an invitation or an opportunity that is moving you in the direction of your vision?

PRACTICING PEACE

CHAPTER 17

WELCOMING PEACE

*The early church began with a tremendous
burst of creative energy, finding, in the
proclamation of the crucified Jesus as the living
Lord, the key to unlock the prison of human
existence.*

N. T. WRIGHT, *THE CONTEMPORARY
QUEST FOR JESUS*

We didn't have many cold nights where I grew up in coastal
Southern California, but evenings at the beach could
be chilly and windy. That's why we had firepits, of course—to
warm ourselves against the moist, inhospitable air while making s'mores. One night, shivering, with damp towels wrapped
around us, we walked to the parking lot, looking forward to
getting out of the breeze and into the car, where we could turn
on the heater.

Turning the key, I heard that dreaded sound: *click-clickety-
click.* Dead battery. I quickly jerked my head around to see if my

friends had left. They had not. I shouted out the window, "Wait, we need a jump!"

Several cars came our way, and thankfully someone had jumper cables—those simple but remarkable contraptions that allow the energy from a powerful place to be transmitted to a weak, empty place. My dead battery welcomed the charge.

We need to welcome peace as it comes to us from Another Reality, God himself. We need to work with the jumper cables that facilitate our reception of peace.

Transpiration

Peace cannot be conjured up by willpower alone. No authority figure can wag their moral finger and effectively demand someone to act or speak in peace. Information, knowledge, perspectives, case studies, and testimonials about peace and peacemakers are wonderful, but none of them typically bring about lasting peace. For every Nelson Mandela or Baroness Bertha von Suttner (the first woman to win the Nobel Peace Prize), there are seemingly a million haters and abusers.

There must be a solid, animating, and energizing source of peace—a soil in which we can ground ourselves and then, absorbing the nutrients, naturally produce the fruit of peace. The soil is interactivity with the Father, Son, and Spirit. To stimulate our imagination for ways the goodness and peace of God can seep into our character, our souls, our hearts, I will introduce you to the concept of *transpiration*.

Transpiration is the process whereby plants absorb water and mineral nutrients through their roots and then give off water vapor through pores in their leaves. Transpiration can be imagined by thinking of water moving up a straw or of liquid being soaked up by a paper towel. This receiving of nutrients in plants results from the action of capillaries that force water up from the ground and disperse it throughout the plant.

We need something like this when it comes to receiving peace. I love the vision of God's life "coming up from the soil" into the "plant" of my life, the way the "capillaries" of the Spirit work against the gravitational pull of our sin and distribute his life for the sake of others into the "leaves" of our lives. How do we give ourselves over to God-based *transpiration*? How do we receive the peace of God such that it flows from us?

Peace, as seen in the blessings of Paul (e.g., Romans 1:7; 1 Corinthians 1:3), is "from God our Father and from the Lord Jesus Christ." It is not something we have to squawk for like a fussy baby looking to be fed. There is no other supplier of peace. Peace is not just a temperament or personality trait possessed by some lucky people. The peace that is *from God* flows to one's heart through the cultivation of a real relationship with the true Creator-Lord of the world. Transpiration is the humble submission to a process designed by God.

Peace in the Real World

Peace is not achieved by detachment from the world. Over the millennia, a lot of Christian people and groups have tried detachment, and it's understandable. Of course we are tempted to flee! Escape has the upsides one might imagine for the pursuit of peace—purity from the taints of the world, removal from the stresses of the world, and protection from the disappointments, frustrations, pains, and heartaches of the world. But how does a "plant" that has isolated itself from everyone let peace flow from its leaves so as to bless others?

Isolation is not the best place to grow peace, and it's the worst place to pass peace. For instance, in the parable of the bags of gold, the person who was given one bag hid it and did nothing (Matthew 25:14–30). The rationale for nonengagement was fear based in the belief that the master was a "hard man" (v. 24). In contrast, the men who were given five and two bags, respectively, each went out and engaged with the world and earned double what was given them. They experienced joy in handing the fruit of their interaction to their master.

What do you think was the state of their hearts? The *interactive investors* were likely animated by confidence, joy, and a sense of adventure and peace. The one-bag person was moved by fear, dread, worst-case-scenario thinking, and anxiety. Each was stirred to action by their concept of God. The defining characteristics of our inner being and our manner of being in the world are influenced by what we *really* think about God—not what we've been told to think, or think we should think, but what is gut-level and intuitive and leads to spontaneous, instinctive words and actions. If our image of God is that he is a hard taskmaster, there will be no peace with him, within, or with others—just the anxious burying of a valuable human life.

But what if God is not a "hard man"? What if he is all-wise and is lovingly and purposefully superintending world history—my history? This "God view" gives confidence in God and a hope for the future that in turn funds our ability to invest our lives into others.

Peace is a quality of heart and mind that one possesses imperfectly within the real world. As apprentices of Jesus, we learn from him that it is possible to possess and pass peace in the midst of life's various realities. Jesus wept at the tomb of his friend Lazarus, but his presence meant restoration to life (John 11). The woman at the well, the woman caught in sin, the tax collector in a tree, the tax collector who hosted Jesus for a dinner party, a confused Nicodemus (John 4; John 8; Luke 19; Luke 5; John 3)—all would say, "Jesus walked into plenty of drama and agony in my life, but he was present in peace." He did not demand that the situation change before he would consent to being there. He stood in the middle of the world's mess in and with peace. Experiencing deep transpiration by means of his connection to his Father, Jesus was a flowing fountain of peace.

Peace in Lament

Peace does not have to go begging for a place of inclusion. Peace can transform any place, time, situation, or event. It may not change the facts of a matter, but it will change how we engage with the facts. Peace can even be an aspect of lament, of deep pain resulting from life's realities. We can feel more than one thing at a time—for instance, both lament and "the joy of the LORD [that] is your strength" (Nehemiah 8:10). Habakkuk gives all of us who feel buried under a waterfall of negativity a ground of being:

> Though the fig tree does not bud
> and there are no grapes on the vines,
> though the olive crop fails
> and the fields produce no food,
> though there are no sheep in the pen
> and no cattle in the stalls,
> yet I will rejoice in the LORD,
> I will be joyful in God my Savior.
>
> HABAKKUK 3:17–18

Compassion for our broken world drives us to seek personal heart peace and others-oriented peacemaking within the ups and downs of daily life. As our lives unfold, we learn to answer the question, *What do I do in the midst of suffering?* We don't run, escape, or fearfully isolate. We put our face in it—in peace and in confidence that joy and hope will meet us there, that power will be found there, that God is there. God is only present in reality. God cannot be in our fantasies of protecting ourselves from suffering by dodging the world. We must place our confidence in the vision of a new world (Isaiah 2:2–5; 11:6–9; 54:10), in the sure hope that fear will be banished (Zephaniah 3:13) and peace will be set in motion by the Messiah (Zechariah 9:10).

Like every aspect of Christian spirituality, transpiration has an intake organism and an output system. This is the way we come to experience N. T. Wright's notion that "God intends to flood creation with his own love."[1] And I would add peace as an aspect of such love. This then leads to the church's acceptance of its role as peacemakers who "cannot rest content while injustice, oppression and violence stalk God's world."[2] We want the overflow of our peace—its goodwill toward others in words and deeds—to be experienced by the whole world, beginning with our neighbors and our enemies.

God is the source of peace. It flows from him. He wants to give it. While we can never earn the graces of God, we simply do our best to make sure nothing in us is blocking the reception of God's gifts. We want to create receptivity. The next chapter provides some insights for doing just that.

Peace with God: Survey the nature and habits of your heart. Is the peace of God flowing to you? Or does it feel blocked? What can you do to take away the blockages and build conduits for peace to flow from God to you?

Peace Within: Are there things in you that hinder the process of transpiration? Maybe you're too busy? Too unfocused? Clear away some clutter and see if you can open a new pipeline for receiving the life of God.

Peace for the Sake of the World: I've argued that peace does not flow from fearful detachment or from hurt-based isolation. Rather, peace is meant to make us willing and able to be interactive investors in the lives of others. Assess how you're doing in this regard.

CHAPTER 18

PEACE BUILDERS: SABBATH AND POVERTY OF SPIRIT

Return to your rest, my soul,
for the LORD has been good to you.

PSALM 116:7

*D*oing nothing—isn't that just a synonym for death? Even when I try to sit still, my legs shake. More than a few hundred times over the years, my wife has put her hand on top of my bouncing leg and demanded, "Stop! You're shaking the whole table and giving me motion sickness!" Doing nothing is terrifying for some, and impossible for others. Yet "stop" or "do nothing" is the basic definition of Sabbath. It takes a special kind of humility, a certain shape of one's spirit, to walk in that direction. But when we do, we will have constructed a reliable bridge to peace.

Sabbath

Practicing Sabbath as a means to peace is not a moralism; it is not a religious regulation meant to produce guilt in us. As Jesus said, "The Sabbath was made for man, not man for the Sabbath" (Mark 2:27). Sabbath is an invitation into a new reality, to a life that allows pause and rest. This in turn gives us the emotional, relational, and spiritual energy needed to live our lives in peace.

Putting Sabbath into play rescues us from rat-race living and opens new vistas of peaceableness. *Sabbathed* lives teach us to say no to *the culture of now* through unplugging, seeking solitude, and learning to appreciate silence.

But let's be practical: removing ourselves from our normal, connected lives of production and consumption can be unnerving. Yet being scared of "doing nothing" is the surest sign that we need to do this. The best test case for Sabbath resistance is our smartphones. The vast majority of us are unsettled by not having our phone close by, within arm's reach. The thought of going without our phone for a day or two makes many of us uncomfortable. People actually sleep with their phone in their beds. I've heard that the average American checks their phone somewhere between fifty and a hundred times a day. It makes me wonder, *Do I own my phone, or does it own me?*

Underneath being owned by smartphones is a combination of fear of missing out (FOMO) and covetousness. Coveting in the biblical tradition includes "both an attitude of craving and forceful action to secure what is craved."[1] It is a powerful instinct instructing us that we all need to and should get more out of life. We should have more, do more, see more, taste more, travel more. These sorts of things, we think, are what constitute well-being and make for the good life.

But commitment, even addiction, to this lifestyle is what brings frenzied multitasking into play. Each moment must be filled with multiple undertakings in order to implement our drive to be more than we are, to control more than we do, and to evermore extend our power and effectiveness. Such practice yields a divided self, with full attention given to nothing.

In stark contrast, the good life is found in simplicity, in clear focus. The simplicity is in following Jesus. The focus is on life in the kingdom of God as Jesus taught about it and lived it. Living a life anchored in Sabbath allows us to be alert, aware, and loyal. It purifies our fidelity to Jesus and others. It deepens our spiritual commitments and gives us the power and grace to yield our lives to God.

Think of it this way: the music we love contains rests, brief moments of silence. Without these rests, music would not be what it is. It would make no sense to our ears. Without rests, music becomes noise. Without Sabbaths of various sizes and frequencies, our living becomes dying. Living without rests causes the angst many of us feel. It is the source of much anti-peace in our hearts and in our communications with one another.

Today, technologies of all kinds fill the spaces meant for rest. In workplaces of various sorts, the relentless chase for more production at ever-increasing speed banishes rest and drives out contemplation, curiosity, imagination, and dreams—which in turn smothers peace. Without peace, we cannot attain the completeness and wholeness that comprise the good life in God's kingdom.

Without rests, without the good life God intended for humans, we concoct lifeless substitutes of various kinds. We try stimulants or depressants, only to find that they mar the work of God in and through us. We try adding entertainments to our lives, only to discover that they create a whirlwind in which the wind of the Spirit is marginalized.

Seeking peace through the practice of Sabbath is not merely an ethic of moderation or a moralism designed to squelch our lives; it is a profound means of comprehensive devotion to God and neighbor. Sabbath rest and the peace it yields propel us to an unreserved and all-consuming giving of self to God that defines the Christian life. The peace generated by rest allows us to be present to God and to his action in our lives.

The habit of Sabbath, born from deep faith in the provision of God, facilitates rest that no nap can touch. Scripture implores us to "make every effort to enter that rest" provided by God (Hebrews 4:11). Making this effort is the sure sign that we are casting all our anxiety on him and discovering that in fact he cares for us (1 Peter 5:7).

As I've gotten older, I have found that Sabbath points toward surrender. The habit of Sabbath calls me to practice giving up my agenda. The restful and peaceful context of Sabbath allows me to ask, *What does it mean to surrender to God in the last phase of my life? How do I live a balanced life of work and contemplation? How do I give myself to the modesty that will focus my life on thinking deeply about a few important things instead of thinking I have to know something about everything that shows up in my newsfeeds?*

I came to the conclusion that I needed to take some special kinds of Sabbaths. I'll name some here that have been important to me. Using them as idea starters, you may decide you need something similar and can create your own.

I've been trying to learn to take a Sabbath from the tyranny of disordered desires. To help me in this, I use the ancient prayer of Thomas à Kempis that I referred to in chapter 1, working it into my life through frequent contemplation:

> Choose always to have less rather than more. Seek always after the lowest place, and to be subject to all. Wish always and pray that the will of God be fulfilled in thee. Behold, such a man as this entereth into the inheritance of peace and quietness.[2]

I seek deliverance from peace-killing levels of activity by taking a Sabbath from addiction to work. About Sabbath, Dallas Willard wrote, "The command is 'Do no work.' Just make space. Attend to what is around you. Learn that you don't have to *do* to *be*.

Accept the grace of doing nothing. *Stay with it until you stop jerking and squirming.*"[3]

I've also arranged for spaces that enable me to take a Sabbath from being noticed by means of position. Envisioning the testimony of Saint Ignatius has become a part of my mental framework. Alice von Hildebrand wrote:

> When St. Ignatius—against his wishes—was elected first superior of his order, he assigned to himself the task of working in the kitchen. Why? First and foremost, because he wanted to serve and not to be served. Second, he was teaching his sons that a small, mean task done with love can glorify God more than a noble one tainted by vanity.[4]

I've learned that seeking peace requires taking a Sabbath from controlling outcomes. For instance, I do my best to lead well, but as much as possible, I leave others in charge of their lives before God. I try new initiatives or better ways of doing things, but I take a Sabbath from needing things to turn out exactly as I want them to. I give my kids the best and most loving advice I can, but I take a Sabbath from manipulating them. To help me to live into these Sabbath-based practices, I've sat with John Wesley's covenant prayer for many hours:

> I am no longer my own but yours.
> Put me to what you will,
> rank me with whom you will;
> put me to doing,
> put me to suffering;
> let me be employed for you,
> or laid aside for you,
> exalted for you,
> or brought low for you;

let me be full,
let me be empty,
let me have all things,
let me have nothing:
I freely and wholeheartedly yield all things
to your pleasure and disposal.[5]

Poverty of Spirit

The ancient phrase *poverty of spirit* points us to the gateway to a consistent life of peace. At first blush, this seems counterintuitive. Who would seek *poverty* of anything? Who would intentionally cultivate scarcity? Only those who know a kind of life, a quality of life, that is characterized by the experiential knowledge of the provision of God.[6]

Jesus illustrates poverty of spirit with a parable. A Pharisee and a tax collector go to the temple to pray. The Pharisee is an icon of the zealous but misguided practice of religion. The tax collector would have been an ancient meme for a notorious sinner. As the Pharisee prays, he reveals an arrogant, self-righteous heart:

"God, I thank you that I am not like other people—robbers, evildoers, adulterers—or even like this tax collector. I fast twice a week and give a tenth of all I get."

But the tax collector stood at a distance. He would not even look up to heaven, but beat his breast and said, "God, have mercy on me, a sinner."

LUKE 18:11–14

Poverty of spirit, while not an everyday phrase, is very much like something you already have a pretty clear idea about—namely, an attitude of humility. Poverty of spirit prepares fertile soil in the soul in which humility, meekness, and contriteness of heart can grow. This attribute is fundamental to all who sincerely seek peace.

Poverty of spirit is "an emptying of self so that God can fill us with life and love."[7] It means we embrace daily dependence on God for all we need. It is rooted in a strong, natural, utter dependence on God. It is based on the firsthand experience that God as Creator cares for us as his creatures. It means we are set free from inordinate attachments to things so we can become free to serve others.

We see an awareness of poverty of spirit in Jesus' confession that he is "gentle and humble in heart" (Matthew 11:29). Paul understands how the intentional self-emptying of spiritual poverty leads to peace for the world: "Being in very nature God, [Jesus] did not consider equality with God something to be used to his own advantage; rather, he made himself nothing by taking the very nature of a servant . . . He humbled himself by becoming obedient to death—even death on a cross!" (Philippians 2:6–8).

The poverty of self-emptying leads to a spiritual fullness that enriches others. God blesses those who seek humility and poverty of spirit: "These are the ones I look on with favor: those who are humble and contrite in spirit" (Isaiah 66:2). John the Baptist lived in harmony with notions of poverty of spirit: "He [Jesus] must become greater; I must become less" (John 3:30). Paul picks up on how the peace-filled spirit of self-emptying spreads for the good of others: "It is for freedom that Christ has set us free . . . But do not use your freedom to indulge the flesh; rather, serve one another humbly in love" (Galatians 5:1, 13).

Contentment and peace work together to strengthen each other—the more content one is with what they have in goods and control, the more peace-filled they are. The more peaceful one is within themselves, the more content they tend to be when it comes to the things of earth. Contentment comes from within, not from circumstances; it is a posture of the heart at rest in humility.

But some of us don't like the concept of dependence—the word alone can trigger panic. Some of us have worked our whole lives to make sure we never have to be dependent on anyone for anything. Reliance on someone else is the scariest thing possible. It suggests weakness and vulnerability. It calls for admitting we are not in control of every person and every moment of life. To live in poverty of spirit and to experience the peace that flows from it, we must be honest about our fear of dependence and face it head-on, not as religious moralism but as a condition of the heart, mind, will, and emotions.

What Do You Want?

Achieving peace usually includes moderating certain elements of our lifestyles. We have to deal with extremes of all kinds. We have to banish any compulsion toward consumption. We have to drop argumentativeness. Compulsive overactivity and hectic stimulation are the precursors of a frenzied mind.

The idea of *moderation* always raises the question, *What do I really want?* Poverty of spirit and its child—peace—or something else? When Jesus told the parables of the treasure hidden in a field and the pearl of great value (Matthew 13:44–46), he had in mind to bring about in his listeners clarity of desire and intention. To paraphrase, Jesus wondered, then and now, *What is of utmost value to you—life in the kingdom of God as an apprentice of Jesus? Or is it the mad pursuit of worldly treasures?*

Poverty of Spirit and Leadership

Modern life sends meekness flying to the curb so that other, "more important" things can hastily push by en route to getting their prizes: power, consumption, and production. But godly leaders, those who radiate spiritual poverty and humility, are meek—they have gentle, peaceful strength that they put to godly use. Consider these examples:

- The Bible says this about Moses: "Moses was a very humble man, more humble than anyone else on the face of the earth" (Numbers 12:3). He knew the direct provision, influence, and care of God in his life. This made him free—not perfect, but free enough to be the meekest person known to mankind. The meek are not weak. They have strong confidence in God and his kingdom—a confidence that is humble, not arrogant, since it is rooted in the person and care of God. These kinds of leaders do not need to strive or grasp, quarrel or cling. They get things done—sometimes big things, like delivering a people from bondage.
- Jesus said, "Blessed are the meek"—happy and to be envied are such people (Matthew 5:5).
- Jesus said of himself, "I am gentle and humble in heart" (Matthew 11:29). Doing his work within the fellowship of the Holy Trinity, Jesus did not have to shove things and people along. He could obediently *be* and unassumingly leave all outcomes to God.
- Jesus wasn't the type of person to "quarrel or cry out . . . [or obnoxiously make known] his voice in the streets" (Matthew 12:19). Instead, as Peter admired about Jesus and commended to others, "When they hurled their insults at him, he did not retaliate; when he suffered, he made no threats. Instead, he entrusted himself to him who judges justly" (1 Peter 2:23).
- Jesus was so deeply committed to using power to serve others that "he got up from the meal, took off his outer clothing, and wrapped a towel around his waist. After that, he poured water into a basin and began to wash

his disciples' feet, drying them with the towel that was wrapped around him" (John 13:4–5).

These examples reveal an unpretentious poverty of spirit and a winsome humility. Taken together, they are a vision for implementing poverty of spirit by *putting ourselves in our rightful place* so we can *take our place* in the story of God.

Having learned that peace comes to us from God and having named some ways we can cooperate with the process of receiving God's peace, in the next chapter, we turn our attention to nurturing peace in our social relations.

Peace with God: An aspect of peace with God is living within the rhythm and values he establishes. How do you do with keeping Sabbath and seeking poverty of spirit? What must change for you to come into alignment with God in these areas?

Peace Within: Try to identify any underlying issues that make practicing Sabbath or poverty of spirit difficult for you. How do you feel led to begin?

Peace for the Sake of the World: Look back at John Wesley's covenant prayer. If it is in line with the desires of your heart, make it into your own prayer, with an emphasis on how it can empower you to be a person of peace for the sake of the world.

CHAPTER 19

PEACE IN SOCIAL RELATIONS

*Almighty God, from whom all thoughts of
truth and peace proceed: Kindle, we pray
thee, in the hearts of all men the true love of
peace; and guide with thy pure and peaceable
wisdom those who take counsel for the nations
of the earth; that in tranquillity thy kingdom
may go forward, till the earth is filled with the
knowledge of thy love; through Jesus Christ our
Lord. Amen.*

BISHOP FRANCIS PAGET, "A
PRAYER FOR PEACE"

It was late in the evening my time (Eastern Standard Time). I
sat on the floor of the dark entryway to our home, the landline
phone on the floor next to me. I was mulling over, for the ump-
teenth time, when I should dial the number for an important call
to the West Coast.

I had come to a proverbial Y in the road. I had to choose what
to do with a big idea. Having started my first church a couple

years earlier, I was now in my mid-twenties and had received a vision for planting twenty churches in the industrial Midwest over the next ten years. The idea sounded grandiose, even to my own ears. When I daydreamed about telling my mentor, I imagined him saying in reply, *Just finish getting your current church off the ground, and call me back when you grow up.*

We must pay attention to big ideas. We must cultivate them, nourish them, and grow in confidence about them. But they have no impact until we take them public. So I finally put the phone on my lap and dialed the number. I heard the familiar voice of my cherished mentor and took my idea public for the first time. "John," I said, "I think God is telling me to plant twenty new churches in the next ten years." "Great!" he replied. "That's wonderful!" Now it was not just the crazy idea of a young leader. It was affirmed. I owned it. I had to put it into practice in public.

Throughout this book, we've been exploring a vision for peace with God, peace within, and peace for the sake of the world. Now it's time to think about how to take this vision public in our everyday relationships. In this chapter, we'll consider three aspects of this task: loving one's enemies, being agents of unity, and practicing civil discourse.

Love Your Enemies

First of all, what do we mean by love? What are its attributes? One of the apostle Paul's most celebrated passages gets us started on the road of what the verb *love* does to its object—*an enemy.*

> Love is patient, love is kind. It does not envy, it does not boast, it is not proud. It does not dishonor others, it is not self-seeking, it is not easily angered, it keeps no record of

wrongs. Love does not delight in evil but rejoices with the truth. It always protects, always trusts, always hopes, always perseveres.

Love never fails.

1 CORINTHIANS 13:4–8

The discussion and disputes we have about important aspects of life—politics, religion, race relations, gender and human sexuality issues—are frequent enemy makers. Conversations about these topics would take place in a completely different atmosphere if they were animated by love. But we cannot just tell each other, "Do what Paul says." The intent of the passage is not a string of moral commands: "Be patient," "be kind," and so forth. Rather, the idea is that those are the things love does: love is patient, kind, not boastful, not proud. The gist of the passage is this: *be filled with God's love such that the traits Paul lists are the natural overflow of our lives.*

But this raises a further question: How do we become filled with God's love? First, stop listening to and viewing hate. Refuse to be drawn to its false certainty, its anger, its condescending attitude, its belittling of others' points of view. The purveyors of animosity are like the producers of the freak shows of old: they use the broken things in the world to get eyeballs and clicks and the profits that come with them. Don't be complicit in their scheme. Love will die in you. Suspicion of others and cynicism toward life will grow. You won't find peace or love of others there. And besides, you have a whole other story to inhabit—namely, becoming the friend of God in the healing of the world.

Second, stop being indifferent. I know modern forms of fear and confusion can drive us in that direction. I feel it myself and truly empathize. But ignoring or abandoning the world is not an option for followers of Jesus. The people and events of our lives are important. They make our lives as we know them. We are a *this-world* people. We join God, who is already here serving the people of this world. Furthermore, our world, with all its sin and damage of creation, is still a God-infused world. His presence in us and in the world is our strength and courage, as well as the grounds for hanging in with a compassion that makes us vulnerable to disappointment.

Third, God is love, so seek him. Get to know him. Let him flow through you. Then Paul's vision will begin to come true. We want to receive what Romans 5:5 proclaims: "God's love has been poured out into our hearts through the Holy Spirit, who has been given to us." Love is not a doctrine to be grasped by the mind; love is an experience of the heart. It is as if your heart is a vessel that the Holy Spirit is pouring liquid love into. This love is for anyone who wants to receive it, wherever you are, just as you are. It can be poured into a broken heart, a needy heart, a fearful heart. All you have to do is open your heart. God's love will lead to a way of knowing that is infused with love, which in turn will lead to peace between persons.

As a general term for seeking to bring about good things for others, love contains a special focus: love for one's enemies. Seeking a life of relational peace means we must face full-on one of the most provocative teachings of Jesus: "Love your enemies, do good to those who hate you, bless those who curse you, pray for those who mistreat you . . . Do good to them, and lend to them without expecting to get anything back . . . Be merciful, just as your Father is merciful" (Luke 6:27–28, 35–36).

What? You've got to be kidding! How is that possible? How is it even good or right? Enemies are hated, despised, and disposed of, right?

Loving our enemy does not mean burying feelings or denying observations. Are there times in life when peace is not the natural, appropriate response? Yes—such as when we resist evil and stop injustice. Jesus spoke out about bad religious leaders (Matthew 23). He overturned the tables of the money changers in the temple (Matthew 21:12). But he did these things from a heart marked by graciousness and love. Even as he took strong, provocative action, he was working for the good of his Father and therefore for the ultimate good of every person. Note, he was *acting*; he wasn't *reacting* in an out-of-control way. Being fully in control, he was making a specific point and acting under the inspiration and supervision of his Father.

Are aggression and conflict ever the best course of action for us? Can we rightly take offense at things? Is conflict sometimes necessary? Yes, but an automatic setting aside of all forms of goodwill in favor of all modes of fighting is completely overblown and overused in human affairs. In our highly divided nations, any important situation can evoke anger, retaliation, bitter conflict, and brutal attacks on others.

Each of us occasionally gets angry and loses our sense of inner peace. The spiritual growth we seek does not erase our humanness; rather, it puts humanness in a new context—namely, one in which we are accompanied as humans by the person and work of the Holy Spirit, who produces fruit in us (Galatians 5:22–23). Repressing anger or aggressive impulses, hiding feelings of hostility, beating ourselves up about anti-peace emotions, or engaging in self-alienation is never the long-term solution. The ultimate strategy for loving one's enemy is patient spiritual transformation into Christlikeness so that anxiety and conflict do not dominate our lives. We don't want our source of confidence for dealing with everyday life to be, "I know I can control you with my anger!"

A person of peace can be forthright without being bitter. A person of peace can be fully present to angry or anxious situations. In fact, when it comes to dealing with enemies, anything that can be achieved by anger, anxious motivations, or overly aggressive means can be done better from a heart at peace, no matter what outward word or action is called for.

To become the kind of person who can deal with tough situations that involve an enemy, we need to adopt a peaceful temperament. Think of such a temperament in terms of natural, consistent patterns of climate. For instance, it's no secret that San Diego, California, has remarkably stable daytime temperatures year-round. Temperatures vary from 66 degrees in the winter to 76 degrees in the summer. We would call that a moderate climate. On the contrary, I spent a good number of years living near Boise, Idaho. The hot and cold temperatures there can show extreme fluctuations in a given year between 10 degrees and 110 degrees.

We are similar. Our souls have a climate, a temperament—hot, cold, calm, indifferent, warm. Some run hot and angry; others run gentle and peaceful. Some of this is in our psychological and spiritual DNA, but unlike physical DNA, our current inward bent is not ultimately determinative. It can be changed under the direction and power of the Spirit. The questions we must ask ourselves are: *Do I want to change? Would I like to be at peace with God, at peace within myself, and a person of peace for the sake of the world? What in my current structure of desire prevents this? What facilitates it? How can I feed the one and starve the other?*

What we're aiming for is an overall climate of peace within our souls. Within this overall soul atmosphere we will have moments not marked by peace. Some of these will result from the sinful bits of our souls; others, like car crashes, stock market crashes, and relational clashes, happen to us, threatening us in powerful ways. We want to develop proper responses to these situations so that when a clear word—or decisive action that is unpleasant to others—is needed, it will flow from a heart otherwise at peace. Peace will make a challenging word more tolerable for others. Peace will assure that a tough action has the most effective outcome.

When we have to deal with nonpeaceful situations where we have perceived or real enemies, we want to do so by means of knowledge, wisdom, and discernment given as gifts of the Spirit. Filled with and guided by the Spirit, we avoid these anti-peace expressions:

- "I gave her a piece of my mind. Who cares what it might do to her!"
- "I let him have it! I'm hoping it does indeed bruise him!"
- "I didn't hold anything back. I gave her the whole dump truck!"

To be good at modeling peace among people, we want to nurture this desire in our hearts, as expressed by Adrian van Kaam: "[Lord,] teach us how to rule aggression instead of being ruled by it . . . May anger surge at the right time, come out the right way as your anger did."[1]

Coming to love our enemies and using aggression only in proper contexts lead to the next aspect of taking peace public— namely, living in unity with others.

Be an Agent of Unity

A lack of division and the presence of unity within one loving, peace-filled, peace-passing people is a key vision found in the New Testament. Unity is one reason the Scriptures emphasize forgiveness, compassion, humility, harmony, and love. The apostle Paul succinctly captures the vision and our part in it:

Make every effort to keep the unity of the Spirit through
the bond of peace.

EPHESIANS 4:3

Live in harmony with one another. Do not be proud, but
be willing to associate with people of low position. Do not be
conceited.

ROMANS 12:16

Furthermore, the complete eternal peace among the Trinity,
expressing itself among human life, is our model for peace in the
world. The unwavering orientation of the persons of the Trinity
to one another is love. Each member wills the good of the whole
Trinity. Their mode of being is primarily revealed to us in the
coming of Jesus and the way he interacted with his Father. The
sending of the Spirit is intended to enable a similar relationship
between the church and the Trinity. At the end of his life, Jesus
is aware that Trinitarian love and unity are crucial to the eras
to come. His passionate prayer has called many generations to
a unity from which peace flows: "I pray also . . . that all of them
[my followers] may be one, Father, just as you are in me and I am
in you. May they also be in us so that the world may believe that
you have sent me . . . I in them and you in me—so that they may
be brought to complete unity" (John 17:20–21, 23).

Jesus' prayer for unity issues from and reflects the loving
unity and communal relations within the Trinity. The manner
in which the members of the Trinity love and honor each other is
a crucial aspect of what it means for us to be made in the image
of God. The Holy Trinity is the ideological and practical grounds
of and the model for peace. No one pictures the Trinity in even
the slightest bit of anxious strife.

Theologians differ in their opinions about whether a hierarchy exists within the Trinity. Scriptures can be cited for both points of view. For our purposes, we can identify one reason to think there is no hierarchy among the persons of the Godhead—namely, that one member would never treat another member of the Trinity as less than them. No member of the Godhead would simply be used by the other. Each member would deeply treasure and earnestly cherish the other. Each would be valued and upheld on the basis of who they are. Oneness would dominate without denying the particular.

We can hardly imagine love-based unity among persons on that level. Modern humans, where their civic and economic contexts allow for it, seek *particularity* over *unity* in almost every conceivable way: the logos on our clothes, the brand of our cars, the name of our neighborhood, the status of our university, our favorite social media platform, the stripes or swooshes on our shoes, the donkey or elephant of our political party, our liberal or conservative bents. These particularities are meant to set us apart from each other, to make us unique and detached from *those others*.

All this splitting up into camps, we believe, is meant to make each one of us feel special, valuable, and desired. But does it work? Is it helping humanity? Can it deliver what it promises? What if really being special means going down a completely different path? Can you imagine Jesus walking into a meeting of the Trinity with swooshes on his sandals, while the Spirit, with stripes on his, looks condescendingly at Jesus and mentally parks Jesus in a lesser spot?

There is no good rationale for the practice of condescending behavior—even given the contrary messages that come from the various channels of our dehumanizing social discourse. Yet major aspects of our economy—social media in particular—are built on ensuring that these divisions are consistently implemented and sustained. After all this pulling apart, we then want to come together? Which impulse do you think is holding sway? Where do you see the most energy being expended?

Peace will grow *among* us when it grows *within* us. When we see the vision of Jesus and the Trinitarian love and goodwill from which it flows, we will develop a taste for unity and a distaste for restless friction. An orientation to unity will prioritize reconciling, not shunning; building bridges, not erecting barriers; extending tender grace, not spreading harsh condemnation; welcoming, not excluding. Those attitudes and behaviors would reveal the great hope and goal of Christlikeness. The apostle Peter put it this way:

> His divine power has given us everything we need for a godly life through our knowledge of him who called us by his own glory and goodness. Through these he has given us his very great and precious promises, so that through them *you may participate in the divine nature*, having escaped the corruption in the world caused by evil desires.
>
> 2 PETER 1:3–4, EMPHASIS MINE

Can you see this great dream? We are invited to participate in the divine nature, to share in the inner life of the triune God himself—the love, respect, admiration, and mutual submission of the Trinity. And through this to find peace! The vision is that such participation is the overflow of deliverance from our evil desires, our addictions that the marketeers and the loudmouths of this world exploit to their gain but to the destruction of our souls, our relationships, and all that God created. The New Testament imagines humanity finding its truest, most vital life in the union of Father and Son that Jesus demonstrated, and in the love abounding from their union leading to peace wherever that love flows. Though the daily headlines say otherwise, we are moving toward this reality: "We have gone throughout the earth and found the whole world at rest and in peace" (Zechariah 1:11).

Jesus isn't just spouting high and lofty ideals in his prayer for unity. He sees a practical outcome—namely, that the world would know about divine unity and know that such unity has overflowed in love for the world. Can you hear the heart cry of Jesus? "Father, please let the world know I love them, even as you have loved me!" It takes a lot of spiritual work for me to grasp, even in a partial way, that Jesus loves me the way his Father loves him. It calls for silence and solitude—for many hours spent in contemplative prayer, worship, and study.

The way Jesus' mission continues on earth is through the Spirit's mediation to us of the love and unity of the Trinity. I need to receive Jesus' love, because with it comes peace. Receiving love and peace, based in my confidence that God is overseeing human history, is my only hope for spreading love and peace to the people and in the events of my life. The mission of the church cannot be reduced only to unity, love, and peace. But justice, evangelism, mission, healing, deliverance, and discipleship cannot be done well or for long without being in alignment with the persons and relational practices of the Holy Trinity.

The relational practices of the Trinity are our best bet for practicing the next bit of taking peace public—namely, civil discourse.

Practice Civil Discourse

Much verbal, emotional, and relational injury is done in the name of "important" or "holy" causes. The higher the cause, the easier the justification for horrible behavior. Why does something being "important" mean we have to yell the loudest and gush the most venom? Why can't it mean, "I must give careful consideration to others and their views because they think this is a significant topic too. They have a lot riding on it too." It can. It just takes hav-ing enough confidence in God that you are willing to risk acting with relational, emotional, and intellectual integrity and to leave the overall outcome to him—even though some may meet your expressions of peace with antagonism or even violence.

The other option is the one we find on social media, talk radio, and cable news—and, following their example, in many common settings. How is it that so many of us have tuned our ears to hear these mean-spirited assaults? It is not in anyone's interest to pass on the anger, aggression, and acrimony that radiate from media platforms and produce increasingly harmful cycles of personal and social ruin. Why is this our instinctual choice?

There is an answer to that question. A great deal of the time, we feel abandoned in a scary world. Those on the other side have already engaged us in *war* (a really terrible anti-peace word to describe normal human differences of opinion). So we must arm ourselves as well. And if we're going to fight, we must employ overwhelming force and aggressive tactics to keep from losing. We need the latest, most powerful weapons: nuclear, chemi-cal, tech-disrupting, laser, missile-based—whatever it takes to embarrass, shut down, or annihilate our enemy. The civilian versions are showing contempt, betraying, cheating, carica-turing, demeaning, degrading, dehumanizing, or demonizing. The horrible behaviors we see online cannot happen absent that wretched list. Where can we find love, loyalty, fairness, honesty, and respect—and the peace that flows from these attributes? When we find them, a whole new tone and vocabulary will char-acterize even our most difficult conversations.

The goal of peace among people is that any feelings we express, even difficult ones, will be—as much as is possible—for the ulti-mate good of others. Otherwise, the expression of thoughts and emotions is simply an insecure and self-centered manipulating of our neighbor or enemy rather than a means of cherishing and serving them. It misses the category of "love for others"—that which Jesus said sums up all the Law and the Prophets.

The apostle Paul urged us to "strive for full restoration, encourage one another, be of one mind, live in peace" (2 Corinthians 13:11) and to "make every effort to keep the unity of the Spirit through the bond of peace" (Ephesians 4:3). This is the vision we want to persist toward:

> "Don't pick on people, jump on their failures, criticize their faults—unless, of course, you want the same treatment. Don't condemn those who are down; that hardness can boomerang. Be easy on people; you'll find life a lot easier. Give away your life; you'll find life given back, but not merely given back—given back with bonus and blessing. Giving, not getting, is the way. Generosity begets generosity."
>
> LUKE 6:37–38 MSG

The practices for peace in our relationships are solid and true. But they can get challenged at the point of trials and temptations. Let's look now at how peace is experienced when we feel tested and enticed.

Peace with God: God loves every person with a love we can never fully understand. He causes the rain to fall on the just and the unjust, which means he loves the people you refuse to love. Bring to mind one such person, and work with God to have his heart for that person.

Peace Within: Yielding control of your life is a key way to build peace within. Do you tend to be a controlling person? If so, ask yourself why. What do you really want from your controlling behavior? Ask yourself, *Is being controlling actually working, or is it a triple loser—not working, ruining my relationships, and destroying my inner peace?*

Peace for the Sake of the World: Consider the lack of unity in the church and the world. Call to mind common prejudices and biases. Can you imagine a different scenario: giving the gift of peace, being truly present, seeking healing, forgiving others, not acting out of anger or resentment? Imagine, then, how *your* world and *the* world would change.

CHAPTER 20

PEACE IN TRIALS AND TEMPTATIONS

The Lord gives strength to his people;
the Lord blesses his people with peace.
                                    Psalm 29:11

God is faithful; he will not let you be tempted
beyond what you can bear. But . . . he will also
provide a way out so that you can endure it.
                              1 Corinthians 10:13

My wife was accompanying me on an international work trip—something she rarely did. My mom was watching our only son. Grandma and son had a great relationship and enjoyed each other's company. Imagine our surprise when a scene from a Chevy Chase vacation movie began to unfold.

We had just finished loading the bags into the trunk of the taxi and had kissed my mom and our son goodbye. As we closed the door, the taxi slowly pulled away from the curb. Our son pulled away from Grandma and began running down the street, chasing the taxi with tears streaming down his cheeks as he bellowed, "Don't leave. Mom, Dad, don't leave!" I'm surprised we made it to London with our hearts still beating. Being left behind can be traumatizing.

The Twelve were on a steep learning curve—so maybe we should give them a break. A clear example of misunderstanding occurred when Jesus told the apostles that they were being left behind, that Jesus was "going away" (John 8:21; 14:28; 16:7). What could this mean? Going where? We can imagine Jesus' friends agonizing over this statement and thinking, *Why would you go away? What could be more important than being with us?*

Jesus, in a typical act of grace, meets the disciples where they are—in their confusion—and explains what is going on. His last words on the topic were these: "I have told you these things, so that in me you may have peace. In this world you will have trouble. But take heart! I have overcome the world" (John 16:33).

Let's look now at how peace companions us in our troubling episodes of trial and temptation.

Trials

Trials come into every life. At some point, misery worms its way in. Trials run the gamut from annoying aches to serious suffering. Trials test us relationally, mentally, emotionally, and spiritually. We're afraid we can't bear them. Anxiety sets in as we question when the trial will end. We wonder if normal will ever return. We feel weak from wrestling with these thoughts. We forfeit the peace we are invited to possess in Jesus, not in the trials themselves. Outside of the peace of Jesus, we become agents of anger and anxiety. And so the world goes, round and round. Some percentage of us seem to continually suffer trials, temptations, and tribulations.

And some percentage have a virus called "anxious anger," which gets passed on in sour attitudes, hurtful words, and mean deeds.

Peter wrote to a church in which Jewish Christians were suffering persecution. Peter had experienced trials, temptations, and suffering and had learned to face them with gentle, calm, confident peace. And so he wanted to encourage those he loved and cared for not to lose hope, to remind them that the risen Christ was with them.

Peter was realistic about trials. He knew that suffering comes to us all and that we should "not be surprised at the fiery ordeal that has come on you to test you, as though something strange were happening to you" (1 Peter 4:12). But neither should we wallow it, sinking into a quicksand of unbelief and despair. Peter recognized both the reality of trials and our ability to persevere in peace in the midst of them. He encourages his friends in their trials by giving them the vision that they have an inheritance in heaven, "though now for a little while you may have had to suffer grief in all kinds of trials" (1:6).

James's take on trials seems unreasonable at first glance. He says to "consider it pure joy . . . whenever you face trials of many kinds" (James 1:2). Most people I know (myself included) stumble over this verse when we first read it. *Consider trials to be pure joy? Why would anyone do that? It doesn't even seem possible.*

The *why* is rooted not in the experience of the trial but in the result of the trial, in what the trial yields. James taught his audience to consider trials a joy "because . . . the testing of your faith produces perseverance" (1:3). This spiritual process does not work when the highest goal of one's life is to avoid pain. And to seek to avoid pain is completely natural.

So what are we to make of this? James is saying that giving ourselves to trials rightly can lead to spiritual growth. They test our faith. They reveal where we really are as followers of Jesus. Once a test has been performed, we can respond to what was revealed. A slight fever from an infection can be lowered with acetaminophen or treated with antibiotics. An old, weak foundation for a home can be structurally reengineered. At the auto repair shop, an engine test reveals the work that has to be done by a mechanic.

Thus the perspective James wants us to grasp is this: Don't run from trials. Notice and name them. Read the test results, and respond in a way that corrects our soul. Patience may need to be applied. We will need to choose peace. I know it's easier said than done—especially when the trials are harsh and chronic. Yet I believe it's true that persevering with a good attitude will produce the peace we need to hang on when things seem unbearable. Paul's view of trials harmonizes with James's understanding. Paul taught, "Be joyful in hope, patient in affliction, faithful in prayer" (Romans 12:12). That is the way we "let perseverance finish its work so that [we] may be mature and complete, not lacking anything" (James 1:4).

Temptation

Temptation is not the same thing as trials. But it has one thing in common: it is everywhere—both inside us and coming at us from outside. The experience of persistent temptation can lead to mental, emotional, and spiritual suffering. James helps us get clear on temptation, explaining that "each person is tempted when they are dragged away by their own evil desire and enticed" (James 1:14).

One common mistake we make is to think we must fight temptation. James's brilliant insight is that we can't fight temptation directly; instead, we must cut off its supply lines of *evil desire*. We cannot be tempted to pursue something we don't already want. So to stubbornly engage in battle against temptation just makes you a person of war, of anti-peace. Rather, we can peaceably work with the Holy Spirit to reorder our wants, our honest desires, that which entices us.

We see our *want* at work in Paul's words to Timothy: "Those who *want* to get rich fall into temptation and a trap and into many foolish and harmful desires that plunge people into ruin and destruction" (1 Timothy 6:9, emphasis mine). Paul depicts the power of desire in human temptation by conveying strong images: we *fall*; we get *trapped*—trapped by *foolish* and *harmful* enticements that *plunge* us (like drowning) into *ruin* (the disintegration of our person) and *destruction* (with devastating consequences). This is why James is concerned that we guard against getting the ball of desire rolling. That way, "desire cannot conceive; it cannot give birth to sin—sin that when full-grown gives birth to death" (James 1:15, my paraphrase).

The work to curb temptation indirectly through the transformation of desire must be pursued diligently and can be done in gentle, patient peace. And it is effective. It will cut off temptation before it can harm you. So don't fight death; cultivate life. Don't yell at the darkness; stand in the light. Light and life have a particular set of desires attached to them—cherishing God and treasuring neighbors and enemies. Cherishing and treasuring naturally sideline the vast majority of common temptations, doing so in peace, which in turn spreads peace throughout the world.

You may need a shot of confidence to cultivate peace while you engage in the process of rearranging your desires. Paul's words in Scripture have given imagination and courage to Christ followers for millennia: "God is faithful; he will not let you be tempted beyond what you can bear. But when you are tempted, he will also provide a way out so that you can endure it" (1 Corinthians 10:13).

A fruitful spiritual practice for avoiding temptation is to add this request to your daily prayer: "And lead us not into temptation, but deliver us from the evil one" (Matthew 6:13). Picture the prayer this way: "Lord, get me off the assembly line of desire before my cravings or the evil one make it too late."

Cultivate an imagination for praying without anxiety, asking God to give you his peace so you can work around your confusion and to help you settle down by letting you know he is watching over you in your times of trial, temptation, and tribulation. My imagination for this comes from the apostle Paul: "Do not be anxious about anything, but in every situation, by prayer and petition, with thanksgiving, present your requests to God. And the peace of God, which transcends all understanding, will guard your hearts and your minds in Christ Jesus" (Philippians 4:6–7).

When life gets bumpy with trials and tribulations, "cast your cares on the LORD and he will sustain you; he will never let the righteous be shaken" (Psalm 55:22). When trials feel like they're leading to a death drop of tribulation, hang on for dear life to the worldview of Paul, who experienced and overcame vastly more tribulations than most of us have or ever will:

> Who shall separate us from the love of Christ? Shall trouble or hardship or persecution or famine or nakedness or danger or sword? . . . No, in all these things we are more than conquerors through him who loved us. For I am convinced that neither death nor life, neither angels nor demons, neither the present nor the future, nor any powers, neither height nor depth, nor anything else in all creation, will be able to separate us from the love of God that is in Christ Jesus our Lord.
>
> ROMANS 8:35, 37–39

If Paul were looking over my shoulder now as I type, he might say to me, "And tell them that 'whatever you have learned or received or heard from me, or seen in me—put it into practice. And the God of peace will be with you . . . And the peace of God, which transcends all understanding, will guard your hearts and your minds in Christ Jesus'" (Philippians 4:9, 7).

These passages of Scripture are an invitation to rest in God in the midst of trials and temptations. The promise of countless testimonies in the Scriptures and throughout the history of the church is that as we arrange our lives to experience deep contentment, joy, and confidence in our everyday lives with God, we experience a pervasive inner transformation of the will, heart, and soul. We are at peace. We are peacemakers.

We turn now to our concluding thoughts, which will help us put into practice what we have learned with *a beginner's mind*. We will answer one last big question about peace and see the revelation of a compelling vision of ultimate peace.

Peace with God: God is actively at work in the suffering we endure in trials and temptations. Finding the goodness of God in these moments rather than accusing him is a key to having peace with him. How would you assess yourself in this regard? Do you tend to be an accuser of God? If so, ask him to help you see him at work in the difficult moments of life.

Peace Within: Peace within requires patience in affliction (Romans 12:12). It also requires a *wanter* who is in control. If you need to work on these things, how can you begin?

Peace for the Sake of the World: People who are centered, grounded, and at peace in the challenging times of life also bring peace to others. Agitated people cannot do this. Ask God to work with you so that you will, for the sake of others, become more peacefully present to hard times and difficult people.

CONCLUSION

O God of unchangeable power and eternal
light . . . by the effectual working of your
providence, carry out in tranquillity the plan of
salvation.

THE BOOK OF COMMON PRAYER

I was in my mid-thirties. Long gone were the trim, strong years when I played college sports. The scale, which I had to lean forward over my belly to see, read 330 pounds! About double what I should have weighed. My frame was not built to carry such weight, especially the knee I had injured during my sports years. And my lower back, which was normally fine, was starting to hurt too. I could feel my normal energy and drive draining away. Being overweight doesn't have a positive effect on one's psyche and confidence either. Our daughter was a newborn, and I wanted to be able to do things with her in the future.

I faced a choice: Would I allow food to master me, or would I step forward into a different lifestyle? Resolute choices must be made on the way to peace. Just as I wanted to lose weight in order to be a good husband and father, a motivation for us as we pursue peace is *for the sake of others*. We need to be aware of the direct connection between conversion and the doctrine of election. To be elect is to be chosen as an instrument of God, not least as an instrument of peace, justice, and healing. Our growth in peace is possible because we were chosen by God to have and to pass peace.

A Beginner's Mind

In pursuing peace, we want to have a beginner's mind—that is to say, an attitude of openness and eagerness. We want to cultivate curiosity. We want to set aside preconceptions and restrictions that have not produced peace and open ourselves to new perspectives, new possibilities.

We want to bring childlike joy to our effort. One day, "[Jesus] called a little child to him, and placed the child among [his disciples]. And he said: 'Truly I tell you, unless you change and become like little children, you will never enter the kingdom of heaven'" (Matthew 18:2–3). What is it about a childlike state of mind and heart that Jesus was commending? He seemed to be saying that to enter the kingdom—and, for our purposes here, its peace—we need unpretentiousness, innocence, trust, and a delight in learning new things. When it comes to spiritual growth, if one is willing to become like a child, there are no old dogs who can't learn new tricks.

A Big Question

Is peace *weak*? Will people take advantage of us and run over us if we seek and practice peace? We may fear it will produce an emotional flatness in us. Yet the experience of peace within is strong and full of life, and it works with the full range of other emotions. It makes us fearless in our connections with others. It animates the positive energies of faith, hope, and love. When we are at peace, the diverse aspects of our humanity work in rhythm and harmony like an orchestra:

- Our heart is bent toward God and has well-ordered desires.
- Our soul is unified and whole in its godly pursuits.
- Our mind is alert but nonjudgmental, not constantly playing negative commentary.
- Our bodily strength is fully charged but at rest—ready to be called on to implement the good.
- Our emotions are calm; they don't leash us and drag us down the street like an out-of-control dog.
- Our will is in line with the things that bring peace.

Pulling these elements of our lives together toward peace is the overall process and a principal goal of spiritual transformation into Christlikeness.[1] It takes patient and slow effort. Some *breakdowns* may occur before you have *breakthroughs*.[2]

Peace requires learning to be gentle and kind to yourself while being honest as you commit to move forward in faith. Self-condemnation, in which you are the greatest disappointment of your life, can never lead to peace. Constantly whipping yourself on the basis of flawed motivations—such as perfectionism or the desire to look good to others—simply causes bruises and scars. It never brings about lasting change.

In Christian spirituality, loving yourself is key to finding peace and becoming a peacemaker. What does it mean to love yourself? For many of us, self-love is counterintuitive—an unnatural and unsettling thought. But self-love is important because you cannot be at peace within while judging, condemning, or even hating yourself.

Appropriate, godly self-love begins with honoring yourself as a creation of God, who has a purpose for you. Ephesians 2:10 puts it this way: "We are God's handiwork, created in Christ Jesus to do good works, which God prepared in advance for us to do."

You are God's handiwork. *You* were re-created in Christ Jesus to do the good you dream of doing in the world. Can you love and embrace the work of God in you? If so, you are moving toward humble, "doing good for others" self-love. When you find that you're at a point where you "turn from evil and do good; seek peace and pursue it" (Psalm 34:14), you will know something good is happening in you, something you can quietly celebrate.

Surrendering to your createdness and accepting your creatureliness is the pathway to peace with God. It banishes bitterness; it sets aside self-centeredness and self-criticism; it silences shaming self-talk. Loving the work of God in us positions us to be at peace for the world. Only our real, created selves can do that; our false selves fall apart in the harsh reality of the world. God is always to be found in reality—and that is where he meets us.

Ambassadors of Peace

Throughout this book, we've learned that the Scriptures implore us to both *seek* and *generate* peace, to be agents of positive change. The biblical picture for this peacemaking is *ambassadorship*:

> All this is from God, who . . . *gave us the ministry of reconciliation*: that God was reconciling the world to himself in Christ, not counting people's sins against them. And *he has committed to us the message of reconciliation*. We are therefore Christ's *ambassadors*, as though God were making his appeal through us.
>
> 2 CORINTHIANS 5:18–20, EMPHASIS MINE

Jesus, the Prince of Peace, furthers our imaginations for being persons of peace as he blesses his friends with these words: "Peace be with you! As the Father has sent me, I am sending you" (John 20:21). Peace, being primary, is given before one is sent.

Peace is the basis for being sent. Embedded in *sentness* is the call to be agents of the peace given to us. People in large segments of the church, understanding both the gift and the *sentness* inherent in peace, have for centuries been sent forth from worship with these words: "Go in peace to love and serve the Lord."[3]

"Go! As the Father sent me, so I send you." Can you hear "Go!" with a fresh childlike heart? Go and do the greater things Jesus anticipated (John 14:12). Ask him, with faith and confidence, to help you love and serve in peace. Be filled with the power of the Spirit! Receive the capacity and character of God.

Let these blessings free us from fearful, defensive, and angry interactions. Let them spark instead a joyous, humble, and winsome engagement with culture as God's "sent out to love" people. Love, gentleness, and peace always lead to more permanent change than do hatred, harshness, and conflict.

Here is a wonderful secret: nothing will make you happier, delight you as much, or give you more peace than being obedient to God. Cooperating with your "Psalm 139 self" (chapters 6, 13) enables you to be a generous, gracious, and generative person. It is the basis for forming yourself into Christlikeness. It will equip and empower you to lead in peace in your sphere of influence. Gracious rather than hostile interactions will become the norm. As God's cooperative friend, you will find your engagement with contemporary culture in peace, not fear, to be intuitive. Conformity to the way God has made, chosen, and sent you is the way to a settled, peaceful, calm, and confident life.

Peace will come and will be spread to those you love as you seek purity of heart and a good conscience, as you moderate your longings, reorder your desires, and pursue patience with yourself— all while seeking submission to the will of God. Peace will settle over you and become an umbrella under which others find relief and healing. Seek the love of Jesus and the ability to endure the loss of comfort, and take up your cross in confident assurance and rest.

None of these exhortations are intended to lead to worried, anxious, paranoid lives; rather, they point to *a way of being* in the world, a participation in what God is already doing in us. Remember that grace, mercy, and the covenant faithfulness of God are core to all this. They are the difference-making realities. We are responders, and we must respond. God's gracious faithfulness does not cancel out our human desires or energies; rather, it focuses them.

A Vision of Peace

A prophetic hope for a coming age of peace and justice drives the story of the Bible forward. Justice and peace *will* come. That assurance grounds us in peace in the moments of life that are filled with conflict. For Christians the promise of peace is not based in social theories, partisan politics, politicians, or the winning of wars that are intended to (but fail to) bring peace. Our hope is based in Jesus the Messiah, the Prince of Peace. Jesus brings to bear and passes on to the church the final inbreaking of the universal *shalom* of God—all the well-being we've been describing earlier. The church is called to be an instrument of this peace until peace arrives in all its fullness in the new heaven and the new earth.

As someone who desires to be an ambassador of peace, I keep my eyes on the vision of Micah and work toward it in the small ways available to me:

They shall beat their swords into plowshares,
And their spears into pruning hooks;
Nation shall not lift up sword against nation,
Neither shall they learn war anymore.

MICAH 4:3 NKJV

You don't have to be at war with anyone ever again. You can simply drop your weapons. You never again need to rely on harsh comments, malicious lies, Twitter tantrums, Facebook flaming, or Instagram snarkiness. We are invited into an alternative life: "Strive for full restoration, encourage one another, be of one mind, live in peace. And the God of love and peace will be with you" (2 Corinthians 13:11).

The age of peace was inaugurated at the coming of Jesus. The Spirit has been given, and with him comes peace. The cross of Jesus and the sending and receiving of the Spirit are the source, vision, and power for that which is astonishing: reconciliation, quick and easy forgiveness of one another, commitment to think the best of each other, justice, inclusion, peacemaking. In spite of all evidence to the contrary, the early twenty-first century is not the age of anxiety, conflict, and war. These are imposters that wildly punch themselves out while peace steadily grows and is passed by followers of Jesus.

The world is heading to peace. This is the way I reimagine the messianic promise of Isaiah 11:6–9:

> The perpetrator will live with the victim of injustice,
>> the aggressive will lie down with the gentle,
> the African and the Asian and the North American together;
>> and a little child will lead them.
> The poor will feed with the rich,
>> their young will lie down together,
>> and the suburbanite will eat straw like the city dweller.
> The weak will play near the powerful,
>> and a person who is differently abled will put their hand
>>> into full life.
> They will neither harm nor destroy
>> on all my holy mountain,

for the earth will be filled with the knowledge of the LORD
as the waters cover the sea.

Peace Wins

Such peace appears to be a pipe dream, a fantasy, a delusion. As a way of dealing with accusations from interior or exterior voices, I've come to meditate on the story of Peter, who denied he was one of Jesus' closest followers (Matthew 26:31–35, 69–75). Jesus predicted that as the tribulations of the night unfolded, before the rooster crowed three times, Peter would disown him three times. Peter objected, telling Jesus that maybe *others* would stumble and disown him, but *he* would never be that person! Jesus saw the true inward bent of Peter's heart, to be sure, but he also saw that the enemy was going to "sift" him (Luke 22:31). Jesus knew Peter wasn't capable of keeping his vows, so Jesus assured him, "I have prayed for you" (verse 32).

Peter did indeed disown Jesus three times, and the rooster did crow. And when it did, the eyes of Jesus and Peter locked across the courtyard. Can you imagine Peter's pain, the deflating sense of having let himself and Jesus down, of losing, of caving in? Then they turned to walk away, Jesus heading off to trial and death, and Peter, with sagging head, slouched shoulders, and lifeless eyes, wandering around to who knows where. But not too much time passed before they both ended up on the shore of the Sea of Galilee (John 21:15–19). Jesus restored their relationship, reinstated Peter to good standing, and recommissioned him for his now world-famous ministry.

This is what I tightly embrace as a source of safety, security, and peace: What if Peter's story is symbolic of all human history? What if all the denials, sins, injustices, unrighteousness, conflicts, and anxieties have restoration, the reconciliation of a beach scene, awaiting them? Even as I hear Jesus saying in the midst of disloyalty, "Don't worry, Peter. I know you can't fathom this, but I'll see you on the beach," I wonder if we can hear Jesus say to us, to all humanity seeking him, "I know you can't imagine the world ever being healed and whole, but I'll see you in the new heaven and the new earth."

Peace and love will be there. The healing of the nations will be there. Reconciliation of all warring parties will be there. Full human flourishing will be there. The ability to keep our vows of fidelity to God will be there. We will no longer fight ourselves—desires versus a will conformed to God's will, thoughts and emotions versus true discernment and knowledge. We will take deep breaths. We will be home. And God "will wipe every tear from [our] eyes. There will be no more death or mourning or crying or pain, for the old order of things has passed away" (Revelation 21:4).

And in this difficult time in which we live, while we hope and wait with expectation, may peace be with you! Receive the true and fresh perspective that in the midst of our waiting, "the one who is in you is greater than the one who is in the world" (1 John 4:4).

Peace wins.

Dear Reader,

You've finished the book. Now what?

Let's keep walking together on the journey to deep peace. Join a new community I designed for peace-seekers like you.

THE CENTER FOR
FORMATION
JUSTICE
AND PEACE

- Take our 10-Day "Deep Peace Challenge" and live into your dream of becoming a person of peace.
- Create a Rhythm of Life that activates you for justice and peace.
- Learn from inspiring, modern-day heroes on our monthly "Peace Talks."

I would be delighted to have you as a companion on the road to deep peace.

Learn more at FormedWell.org

GRATEFUL ACKNOWLEDGMENTS

M y first thanks in any book always goes to my wife of forty-three years, Debbie. She is my lifelong partner and my biggest supporter. She unfailingly and without complaint is patient with my after-hours and weekends of writing.

I also want to think J. D. Walt (Seedbed, New Room) for helping shape the vision for this book as one component of sowing for a great awakening. Andrea Bailey Willits, the director of communications for my diocese—Churches for the Sake of Others (C4SO)—is always an invaluable source of editorial help. Lisa Pompa, my sister and assistant, was a tireless defender of my calendar, making sure I had time to fulfill my main duties while also finding slots during which I focused on writing. My colleague, Rev. Karla Stevenson, read the first draft of the book and suggested many difference-making changes.

It was a pleasure to publish for the first time with Zondervan. Everything in the book was made better by Ryan Pazdur, associate publisher and executive editor. Steve Norman assisted in the editing at the early stages. Dirk Buursma is a consummate copy editor, who, while being faithful to my thoughts and voice, makes my writing sharper, thus enhancing the experience of the reader. Zondervan Reflective's vice president of marketing Jesse Hillman and senior marketing manager Nathan Kroeze provided outstanding counsel and support in all things marketing. All of these people and their teams are true experts.

Finally, thanks must go out to the clergy, staff, and leaders of my diocese. They exhort their bishop to be a teaching bishop. Their vision and generosity give me the bandwidth to do so.

NOTES

Introduction

1. Experiencing occasional stress or even anxiety is human, and it's normal. It is not something to judge yourself for or to be overly concerned about. It's only when stress becomes chronic or when one has recurring and severe episodes of anxiety that can turn into anxiety disorders or panic attacks that it's time to see a doctor or therapist about it. In this book, the peace we seek makes a welcome contribution to any level of stress. Other forms of healing, both medicinal and therapeutic, may be warranted. I am making no medical claims nor giving any medical advice. I am advocating for the spiritual reality, practical daily benefit, and missional effect of peace with God, peace within, and peace for the world. According to the Mayo Clinic, you should see a doctor when:

   - You feel like you're worrying too much and it's interfering with your work, relationships, or other parts of your life.
   - Your fear, worry, or anxiety is upsetting to you and difficult to control.
   - You feel depressed, have trouble with alcohol or drug use, or have other mental health concerns along with anxiety.

- You think your anxiety could be linked to a physical health problem.
- You have suicidal thoughts or behaviors; if this is the case, seek emergency treatment immediately.

2. See H. Beck and C. Brown, "Peace," in *The New International Dictionary of New Testament Theology*, ed. Colin Brown (Grand Rapids: Zondervan, 1986), 2:777.
3. See Charles L. Feinberg, "Peace," in *Evangelical Dictionary of Theology*, ed. Walter Elwell (Grand Rapids: Baker Academic, 2001), 833.
4. See Dale W. Brown, "Peace," in *The New Dictionary of Christian Ethics and Pastoral Theology*, ed. David J. Atkinson et al. (Downers Grove, IL: InterVarsity, 1995), 655.
5. See Feinberg, "Peace," 833.
6. See Dennis P. Hollinger, "Mission and Ministry," in *Dictionary of Christian Spirituality*, ed. Glen G. Scorgie et al. (Grand Rapids: Zondervan, 2011), 658.
7. Beck and Brown, "Peace," 2:781.
8. Beck and Brown, "Peace," 2:781. The mark of the Stoics is to ignore externals in favor of developing inward strength so as to bear with life through indifference and self-control.
9. When it comes to issues of race, awareness of *tone policing* is crucial. Tone policing is steering or shutting down the stories, statements, or arguments of people of color because of the tone in which they are expressed. When oppressed persons are telling their stories, they are permitted to express them with their genuinely felt attending emotions.

Chapter 1: Peace Killers: Fear, Anger, Aggression, Attachments

1. Adrian van Kaam, *Spirituality and the Gentle Life* (Denville, NJ: Dimension, 1974), 57.
2. Thomas à Kempis, *The Imitation of Christ in Four Books*, trans. William Benham (New York: Dutton, 1905), 115.

Chapter 2: Peace Killers: Pain, Unanswered Prayer, Self-Centeredness

1. "Pain Awareness Month—September 2018," *Morbidity and Mortality Weekly Report* 67, no. 36 (September 14, 2018), Centers for Disease Control and Prevention, www.cdc.gov/mmwr/volumes/67/wr/pdfs/mm6736a2-H.pdf.
2. Leon F. Seltzer, "Self-Absorption: The Root of All (Psychological) Evil?" *Psychology Today*, August 24, 2016, www.psychologytoday.com/us/blog/evolution-the-self/201608/self-absorption-the-root-all-psychological-evil.
3. Seltzer, "Self-Absorption."
4. Seltzer, "Self-Absorption," emphasis added.
5. "The Kingdom of God," copyright © 2007, Ateliers et Presses de Taizé, Taizé Community, France GIA Publications, Inc.

Chapter 3: Peace Killers: Life Online, Obsession with Failure, Fear of Missing Out

1. Susan Muto and Adrian van Kaam, *Practicing the Prayer of Presence* (Totowa, NJ: Resurrection, 1993), 158.
2. Ronald V. Wells, *Spiritual Disciplines for Everyday Living* (Red Deer, Alberta: RDC Books, 1987), 61.
3. Adrian van Kaam, *Spirituality and the Gentle Life* (Denville, NJ: Dimension, 1974), 155–56.

Chapter 4: The God of Peace

1. For an introduction to spiritual practices, see Dallas Willard, *The Spirit of the Disciplines: Understanding How God Changes Lives* (San Francisco: HarperSanFrancisco, 1988).
2. Martin Laird, *Into the Silent Land: A Guide to the Christian Practice of Contemplation* (Oxford: Oxford University Press, 2006), 15.
3. See Laird, *Into the Silent Land*, 16.
4. Carolyn J. B. Hammond, ed., *Augustine: Confessions Books 9–13* (Cambridge, MA: Harvard University Press, 2016), 135.
5. See E. J. Schnabel, "Mission," in *Dictionary of Jesus and the*

Gospels, ed. Joel B. Green (Downers Grove, IL: InterVarsity, 2013), 604.

6. See Dennis P. Hollinger, "Mission and Ministry," in *Dictionary of Christian Spirituality*, ed. Glen G. Scorgie et al. (Grand Rapids: Zondervan, 2011), 658.

Chapter 5: The Peace of God's Kingdom

1. See *The Social Dilemma*, directed by Jeff Orlowski; written by Davis Coombe, Vickie Curtis, and Jeff Orlowski (Exposure Labs, 2020), distributed by Netflix.
2. Dallas Willard, *The Divine Conspiracy: Rediscovering Our Hidden Life in God* (San Francisco: HarperSanFrancisco, 1998), 11.
3. "Ten Elements of Ignatian Spirituality," Loyola Press, 2020, www.ignatianspirituality.com/what-is-ignatian-spirituality/10-elements-of-ignatian-spirituality.
4. "Ten Elements of Ignatian Spirituality."
5. "Ten Elements of Ignatian Spirituality."
6. See "Ten Elements of Ignatian Spirituality."
7. See Vinita Hampton Wright, "Consolation and Desolation," Loyola Press, 2017, www.ignatianspirituality.com/consolation-and-desolation-2.

Chapter 6: Choosing Peace with God

1. Quoted in *Prayers Encircling the World: An International Anthology* (Louisville, KY: Westminster John Knox, 1998), 184.

Chapter 7: An Apprentice to Jesus in Peace

1. N. T. Wright, *The Climax of the Covenant: Christ and the Law in Pauline Theology* (Minneapolis: Fortress, 1993), 256.
2. N. T. Wright, *The Challenge of Jesus: Rediscovering Who Jesus Was and Is* (Downers Grove, IL: InterVarsity, 1999), 94–95.
3. Dallas Willard, *Renovation of the Heart: Putting On the Character of Christ* (Colorado Springs: NavPress, 2002), 136.
4. Wright, *Challenge of Jesus*, 161.
5. Wright, *Challenge of Jesus*, 58, italics in original.

Chapter 8: The Jesus of Justice, Mercy, and Humility

1. See *New York Times* staff, "What to Know about the Death of George Floyd in Minneapolis," *New York Times*, March 30, 2021, www.nytimes.com/article/george-floyd.html.
2. Quoted in Richard J. Foster, *Streams of Living Water: Celebrating the Great Traditions of the Christian Faith* (San Francisco: HarperSanFrancisco, 1998), 135.
3. Foster, *Streams of Living Water*, 137.
4. N. T. Wright, *Evil and the Justice of God* (London: SPCK, 2006), 53.
5. Dorothy Day, *The Long Loneliness: The Autobiography of Dorothy Day* (San Francisco: HarperSanFrancisco, 1997), 166.
6. See "CliftonStrengths," Gallup, www.gallup.com/cliftonstrengths/en/252137/home.aspx.
7. Oscar Arnulfo Romero, *The Violence of Love* (Farmington, PA: Bruderhof Foundation, 2003), 24–25, www.romerotrust.org.uk/sites/default/files/violenceoflove.pdf. Used with permission.
8. Romero, *Violence of Love*, 103.
9. Romero, *Violence of Love*, 144.
10. Romero, *Violence of Love*, 201.
11. Romero, *Violence of Love*, 57.
12. Elizabeth O'Connor, *Journey Inward, Journey Outward* (New York: Harper & Row, 1968), 131.
13. O'Connor, *Journey Inward, Journey Outward*, 170.
14. Bruce K. Waltke, *A Commentary on Micah* (Grand Rapids: Eerdmans, 2007), 387.
15. See Waltke, *Commentary on Micah*, 391.
16. Bruce Waltke, "Micah," in *The Minor Prophets: An Exegetical and Expository Commentary*, ed. Thomas Edward McComiskey (1991; repr., Grand Rapids: Baker, 2009), 733.
17. See Walter Brueggemann, Sharon Parks, and Thomas H. Groome, *To Act Justly, Love Tenderly, Walk Humbly: An Agenda for Ministers* (Eugene, OR: Wipf & Stock, 1997), 5; see also Waltke, "Micah," in *The Minor Prophets*, 734.
18. Brueggemann, Parks, and Groome, *To Act Justly, Love Tenderly, Walk Humbly*, 39.

19. Brueggemann, Parks, and Groome, *To Act Justly, Love Tenderly, Walk Humbly*, 15.
20. Brueggemann, Parks, and Groome, *To Act Justly, Love Tenderly, Walk Humbly*, 58.
21. For this insight, I'm indebted to Richard Foster, *Celebration of Discipline: The Path to Spiritual Growth* (New York: Harper & Row, 1978), 107.
22. Foster, *Celebration of Discipline*, 122.
23. Foster, *Celebration of Discipline*, 114, italics in original.
24. Elizabeth O'Connor, *Eighth Day of Creation: Discovering Your Gifts and Using Them* (Waco, TX: Word, 1983), 48.
25. Quoted in O'Connor, *Eighth Day of Creation*, 26.

Chapter 9: The Spirit of Peace

1. From my article "Missional Leadership for the Ordinary Pastor: Three Simple Steps," *Anglican Compass*, February 19, 2020, https://anglicancompass.com/missional-leadership-for-the-ordinary-pastor-3-simple-steps.
2. Dallas Willard, *The Great Omission: Reclaiming Jesus's Essential Teachings on Discipleship* (San Francisco: HarperSanFrancisco, 2006), 28.

Chapter 10: The Spirit of the Lord's Favor

1. See "Invisible Children: Film," https://invisiblechildren.com/program/film.
2. Elizabeth O'Connor, *Cry Pain, Cry Hope: Thresholds to Purpose* (Waco, TX: Word, 1987), 80.
3. N. T. Wright, *Evil and the Justice of God* (London: SPCK, 2006), 98, 104, italics in original.
4. Wright, *Evil and the Justice of God*, 109.
5. Obery M. Hendricks Jr., *The Politics of Jesus: Rediscovering the True Revolutionary Nature of the Teachings of Jesus and How They Have Been Corrupted* (New York: Three Leaves, 2006), 93.
6. Esau McCaulley, *Reading While Black: African American Biblical*

Interpretation as an Exercise in Hope (Downers Grove, IL: InterVarsity, 2020), 94.

7. Eugene R. Schlesinger, *Missa Est! A Missional Liturgical Ecclesiology* (Collegeville, MN: Fortress, 2017), 129.

8. O'Connor, *Cry Pain, Cry Hope*, 31.

9. O'Connor, *Cry Pain, Cry Hope*, 32.

10. Henri Nouwen, *In the Name of Jesus: Reflections on Christian Leadership* (New York: Crossroad, 1989), 67–68.

11. Richard J. Foster, *Streams of Living Water: Celebrating the Great Traditions of Christian Faith* (San Francisco: HarperSanFrancisco, 1998), 175, emphasis mine.

12. O'Connor, *Cry Pain, Cry Hope*, 107.

13. Quoted in Elizabeth O'Connor, *Journey Inward, Journey Outward* (New York: Harper & Row, 1968), 108–9, italics in original.

14. O'Connor, *Cry Pain, Cry Hope*, 83.

15. O'Connor, *Cry Pain, Cry Hope*, 84–85.

16. Hendricks, *Politics of Jesus*, 318.

Chapter 11: Cultivating a Mellow Heart

1. Adrian van Kaam uses the term *mellow* several times in his *Spirituality and the Gentle Life* (Denville, NJ: Dimension, 1974). I had never seen the term before in any of the modern literature on spiritual formation. But given the rage that seems to define our days, I'm captivated by its potential.

2. Van Kaam, *Spirituality and the Gentle Life*, 13.

Chapter 12: Why So Anxious, O My Soul?

1. Adrian van Kaam, *Spirituality and the Gentle Life* (Denville, NJ: Dimension, 1974), 25.

2. See Dallas Willard, *Life without Lack: Living in the Fullness of Psalm 23* (Nashville: Nelson, 2018). Willard explores Psalm 23 from the point of view of spiritual transformation.

3. See "χρηστός [*chrēstos*]," in "Lexicon: Strong's G5543 *chrēstos*,"

Blue Letter Bible, www.blueletterbible.org/lang/lexicon/lexicon.cfm?t=kjv&strongs=g5543; see also Gerhard Friedrich, ed., *Theological Dictionary of the New Testament* (Grand Rapids: Eerdmans, 1974), 9:483–85.

4. Dallas Willard, *Renovation of the Heart: Putting on the Character of Christ* (Colorado Springs: NavPress, 2002), 15.

5. Jonathan Noël, "A Cloud of Peace (Ode 35)," n.d., track 7 on *The Odes Project, Volume 1*, The Odes Project, April 1, 2008, compact disc.

6. The Fray, "Be Still," recorded 2011, track 12 on *Scars and Stories*, Epic Records, February 7, 2012, compact disc and digital.

7. Fernando Ortega, "Grace and Peace," n.d., track 1 on *The Shadow of Your Wings: Hymns and Sacred Songs*, Curb Records, October 24, 2006, compact disc and digital.

8. Horatio Spafford, "It Is Well with My Soul," 1873, public domain; Irish hymn (ca. 1700), "Be Thou My Vision," trans. Mary Elizabeth Byrne, 1905, public domain.

9. For an introduction to breath prayers, see Sharon Lee Song, "Take Time for Breath Prayer," *Christianity Today*, February 6, 2018, www.christianitytoday.com/women-leaders/2018/february/take-time-for-breath-prayer.html.

Chapter 13: Peace for an Anxious Mind

1. Martin Laird, *Into the Silent Land: A Guide to the Christian Practice of Contemplation* (Oxford: Oxford University Press, 2006), 79. I highly commend this section of his book.

2. See Laird, *Into the Silent Land*, 80–89, for helpful ideas along these lines.

Chapter 14: Rejecting Fear-Based Hostility

1. Quoted in Timothy Keller and John Inazu, *Uncommon Ground: Living Faithfully in a World of Difference* (Nashville: Nelson, 2020), 95.

2. I use the word *xenophilia* is its strict sense—"love of the other."

I don't have in mind the way it is now being used to describe various forms of sexual arousal.

3. Eugene Peterson, *Tell It Slant: A Conversation on the Language of Jesus in His Stories and Prayers* (Grand Rapids: Eerdmans, 2008), 70.

Chapter 15: Loving the Other

1. Jeff Horwitz and Deepa Seetharaman, "Facebook Executives Shut Down Efforts to Make the Site Less Divisive," *Wall Street Journal*, May 26, 2020, www.wsj.com/articles/facebook-knows-it-encourages-division-top-executives-nixed-solutions-11590507499.

2. Elizabeth Chang, "Americans Are Living in a Big 'Anger Incubator.' Experts Have Tips for Regulating Our Rage," *Washington Post*, June 30, 2020, www.washingtonpost.com/lifestyle/wellness/anger-control-protests-masks-coronavirus/2020/06/29/a1e882d0-b279-11ea-8758-bfd1d045525a_story.html.

3. "Public's Mood Turns Grim; Trump Trails Biden on Most Personal Traits, Major Issues," Pew Research Center: U.S. Politics & Policy, June 30, 2020, www.people-press.org/2020/06/30/publics-mood-turns-grim-trump-trails-biden-on-most-personal-traits-major-issues.

4. "A *theological* anthropology is an attempt to think through the meaning of the human story as it is lived out before, with, and by God. This orientation does not mean that various accounts of natural and human sciences are not relevant to our understanding of the human being. Such descriptions are provisional versions of human reality that must be deepened by Christian beliefs ("Theological Anthropology: What Is Distinct about a Christian View of the Person?" Fuller Theological Seminary, September 15, 2010, www.fuller.edu/next-faithful-step/resources/theological-anthropology).

5. I don't see the scene in which Jesus overturned the tables of the

money changers (Matthew 21:12) as him "going off." I see it as a dramatic, intense prophetic act. I guess such similar actions are possible for his followers, but I caution us to be very careful. We don't have Jesus' perfections.

Chapter 16: Pursuing Peace with Others

1. See Jan Tullberg, "The Golden Rule of Benevolence versus the Silver Rule of Reciprocity," *Journal of Religion and Business Ethics* 3, no. 2 (January 2012), https://via.library.depaul.edu/jrbe/vol3/iss1/2.
2. "Spirit of the Living God," 1926, lyrics by Daniel Iverson.

Chapter 17: Welcoming Peace

1. N. T. Wright, *What Saint Paul Really Said: Was Paul of Tarsus the Real Founder of Christianity?* (Grand Rapids: Eerdmans, 1997), 164.
2. Wright, *What Saint Paul Really Said*, 164.

Chapter 18: Peace Builders: Sabbath and Poverty of Spirit

1. See Walter Brueggemann, *Sabbath as Resistance: Saying No to the Culture of Now* (Louisville, KY: Westminster John Knox, 2017), 70.
2. Thomas à Kempis, *The Imitation of Christ in Four Books*, trans. William Benham (New York: Dutton, 1905), 115.
3. Dallas Willard, *The Great Omission: Reclaiming Jesus's Essential Teachings on Discipleship* (San Francisco: HarperSanFrancisco, 2006), 36, emphasis added.
4. Alice von Hildebrand, "Should We Be Indifferent to Everything but God?" Catholic Answers, April 1, 2007, www.catholic.com/magazine/print-edition/should-we-be-indifferent-to-everything-but-god.
5. "The Methodist Covenant Prayer," www.methodist.org.uk/about-us/the-methodist-church/what-is-distinctive-about-methodism/a-covenant-with-god.

6. See Dallas Willard, *Life without Lack: Living in the Fullness of Psalm 23* (Nashville: Nelson, 2019).

7. Kevin O'Brien, *The Ignatian Adventure: Experiencing the Spiritual Exercises of Saint Ignatius in Daily Life* (Chicago: Loyola, 2011), 159, www.ignatianspirituality.com/ignatian-prayer/the-spiritual-exercises/poverty-of-spirit.

Chapter 19: Peace in Social Relations

1. Adrian van Kaam, *Spirituality and the Gentle Life* (Denville, NJ: Dimension, 1974), 91.

Conclusion

1. A way to start on the journey is by reading Dallas Willard's *Renovation of the Heart* (Colorado Springs: NavPress, 2002) and James Bryan Smith's *The Good and Beautiful God* (Downers Grove, IL: InterVarsity, 2009) and *The Good and Beautiful Life* (Downers Grove, IL: InterVarsity, 2009). From there, you will discover Henri Nouwen, Richard Foster, and many other guides—Catholic, Orthodox, and Protestant.

2. See Martin Laird, *Into the Silent Land: A Guide to the Christian Practice of Contemplation* (Oxford: Oxford University Press, 2006), 5.

3. Episcopal Church, *The Book of Common Prayer* (New York: Church Hymnal Corp., 1979), 366.

Try these other Seedbed resources...

For The Body
Recovering a Theology of Gender, Sexuality, and the Human Body
TIMOTHY TENNENT

The human body is an amazing gift, yet many downplay its importance and fail to understand what Christianity teaches about our the God-given purposes for our bodies. We misunderstand how the body was designed and its role in relating to others, while also ignoring the dangers of objectifying the body, divorcing it from its intended purpose.

In *For the Body*, author Timothy Tennent explores what it means to be created in the image of God and how our bodies serve as icons that illuminate God's purposes. Looks at how the human body has been objectified in art and media today, Tennent offers a framework for discipling people in a robust theology of the body.

Tennent presents a truly Christian vision of creation that informs our self-understanding, how we treat others, and how we engage today's controversial and difficult discussions on human sexuality with grace, wisdom, and confidence.

Available in:
Hardcover (272 pages)
DVD / Streaming video - Eight Sessions with Timothy Tennent
Video Study Guide - Discussion guide for small group study.

Living Room Liturgy
A Book of Worship for the Home
WINFIELD BEVINS

Worship doesn't just happen within the four walls of a church building; it can also happen in our homes.

Living Room Liturgy is written to help you worship in the everyday moments of life in your home. It contains liturgies and shorter prayers that can be used while enjoying a morning cup of coffee, at the dinner table, while you're spending time with your loved ones in your living room, or in the evenings at your children's bedsides before they fall asleep. Use these liturgies and prayers at your own pace; add songs or additional scriptures, or pray additional prayers. You will find your faith refreshed as you use these liturgies in your everyday life, especially in your home.

Available in:
Hardcover (158 pages, Limited Edition embossed version)

Find these and many more resources now at my.seedbed.com